D0115913

TRADITIONAL
HYMNS

TRADITIONAL
HYMNS

A John Macrae Book

HENRY HOLT AND COMPANY
NEW YORK

Henry Holt and Company, Inc.
Publishers since 1866
115 West 18th Street
New York, New York 10011

Henry Holt® is a registered trademark of Henry Holt and
Company, Inc.

Compilation copyright © 1996 by Ebury Press
All rights reserved

First published in the United States in 1996 by
Henry Holt and Company, Inc.
Originally published in Great Britain in 1996 by Ebury Press.

Library of Congress Catalog Card Number is available
on request.

ISBN 0-8050-4843-X

Henry Holt books are available for special promotions and
premiums. For details contact: Director, Special markets.

First American Edition – 1996

Designed by David Fordham

Picture research by Jenny de Gex
Printed in Singapore

All first editions are printed on acid-free paper.∞
1 3 5 7 9 10 8 6 4 2

CONTENTS

INTRODUCTION

> A verse may find him, who a sermon flies,
> And turn delight into a sacrifice.
>
> (*George Herbert*, 'The Church-porch')

Hymns have been sung to the gods from the earliest times, and it is no surprise that the earliest Christians adopted them in their worship. According to Mark 14:26, Christ and his disciples sang a hymn after the Last Supper, and St Paul exhorted both the Ephesians and the Colossians to teach and admonish one another in psalms, hymns and spiritual songs. Greek hymns were used by the Eastern church in the early centuries of Christianity, and Latin hymns were used by St Ambrose, who introduced them at Milan in the fourth century and is traditionally credited with having written the *Te Deum*. Poets such as Venantius Fortunatus ('Pange, lingua, gloriosi – Sing, my tongue, the glorious battle') carried on the tradition, later continued by Theoduph of Orleans ('Gloria, laus, et honor – All glory, laud, and honour') and Rhabanus Maurus ('Veni Creator Spiritus – Come, Holy Ghost, our souls inspire'). The Celtic church also used hymns, including the magnificent *Lorica* or 'breastplate' of St Patrick.

These Latin hymns disappeared at the Reformation, not to be revived (with a few notable exceptions) until the nineteenth century. In their place the zealous reformers adopted metrical psalms, producing in 1562 *The Whole Booke of Psalmes*, chiefly the work of Thomas Sternhold and John Hopkins. While the metrical form was often clumsy, William Kethe's version of the Psalm 100 showed how it could be solid and strong:

> All people that on earth do dwell,
> Sing to the Lord with cheerful voice:
> Him serve with mirth, his praise forth tell;
> Come ye before him and rejoice.

At the end of the psalm book metrical versions of the *Te Deum*, the *Benedicite*, and other ancient hymns and canticles were printed. This practice suggested the possibility of versifying other passages from Holy Scripture, which were first attempted by George Wither in his *Hymns and Songs of the Church* of 1623. Wither's book caused much controversy; his hymns being described as 'unfit to keep company with David's Psalms'. The singing of psalms in England was only gradually modified – and hardly at all in Scotland – by the introduction of paraphrases or hymns. Benjamin Keach introduced hymn singing in his Baptist congregation probably sometime in the 1670s, and other Puritans, such as John Bunyan and Richard Baxter, wrote devotional poetry in psalm metres. The metre which had been used for Psalm 148 in *The Whole Booke of Psalmes*, 6.6.6.6.4.44.4, was taken up by Baxter for 'Ye holy angels bright', and by Samuel Crossman for 'My song is love unknown'. Crossman, who became Dean of Bristol, was one of a growing number of Church of England hymn writers: earlier in the century John Donne had his 'Hymn to God the Father' (Wilt thou forgive that sin) set to music, and George Herbert, a fine musician, had written devotional poems which have since become much loved as hymns. The eccentric John Mason wrote 'How shall I sing that majesty', and Bishop Ken wrote his simple and direct morning and evening hymns, 'Awake, my soul, and with the sun' and 'Glory to Thee, my God, this night'. These hymns, written originally for schoolboys at Winchester College, are so central to human experience that it is not surprising to find the first of them opening *Hymns Ancient and Modern* in 1861.

George Herbert's lines from 'The Church-porch', quoted at the head of this introduction, encouraged the writing of hymns and sacred poems. By the mid-1690s there had been a good deal of activity both within and outside the Church of England, including a 'New Version' of the psalms by Tate and Brady (Sternhold and Hopkins's book became the 'Old Version') which contained. 'As pants the hart for cooling streams' and the paraphrase 'While shepherds watched their flocks by night'. Then came Isaac Watts, who took the hymn form and gave it new assurance:

> O God, our help in ages past,
> Our hope for years to come,
> Our shelter from the stormy blast
> And our eternal home.

Like Sternhold and Hopkins he uses the straightforward Common Metre, but the words and lines fit it perfectly, each line strong in itself but related to the others, so that the verse too is firm and assured. Watts loved firmness and clarity: that is why his hymn on death, 'There is a land of pure delight', is so moving, because he sees the landscape of heaven so clearly:

> Sweet fields beyond the swelling flood
> Stand dressed in living green; . . .

and it is with grave clarity that he meditates upon the crucifixion:

> See from his head, his hands, his feet,
> Sorrow and love flow mingled down;
> Did e'er such love and sorrow meet,
> Or thorns compose so rich a crown?

Isaac Watts' hymns stimulated others to write, such as his friend Philip Doddridge ('O God of Bethel') and the Baptist Anne Steele, who was the first major woman hymn writer. Watts was included in John Wesley's first book, the Charlestown Collection of *Psalms and Hymns* of 1737. John Wesley was a fine translator of German hymns, but it was his younger brother Charles who became the poet of the Methodist revival. His hymns are packed tight with biblical phrases and filled with a sense of personal drama; sometimes they rise to an intensity that is close to a mystical experience:

> Till we cast our crowns before Thee,
> Lost in wonder, love, and praise.

Charles Wesley's hymns were both evangelical and eucharistic; but in the later eighteenth century the evangelical mode prevailed, with writers such as Augustus Montague Toplady ('Rock of ages, cleft for me') and John Newton ('Glorious things of thee are spoken'). The most sensitive of them, William Cowper, combined self-examination ('O for a closer walk with God') with nature and weather imagery:

> Ye fearful saints, fresh courage take,
> The clouds ye so much dread
> Are big with mercy, and shall break
> In blessings on your head.

The powerful effect of hymn singing upon evangelicals and Nonconformists led Anglicans such as Reginald Heber ('Brightest and best of the sons of the morning') and Henry Hart Milman ('Ride on! ride on in majesty!') to provide hymns for the Church of England, related to the church's year and the *Book of Common*

Prayer. Heber's 'Holy, holy holy!', for example, was written for Trinity Sunday, and 'Brightest and best' was written for the Epiphany (John Keble's *The Christian Year* was structured on the same principle). The result was a great flowering of Anglican hymnody, beginning with Henry Francis Lyte, whose 'Praise, my soul' sings wonderfully and whose 'Abide with me' is a touching expression of human frailty and trust. Lyte's hymns were included in the book which brought hymn singing into the centre of Anglican worship, *Hymns Ancient and Modern*. Its various editions included hymns such as 'Eternal Father, strong to save', 'Onward, Christian soldiers', 'The day Thou gavest', and 'The Church's one foundation'. Its music, under the inspired direction of William Henry Monk, put tunes to hymns that have since become inseparable from them.

Its greatest single contributor was J.M. Neale, whose translations included 'Jerusalem the golden', who presided over a revival of ancient hymnody. Another contributory stream was from the German, translated by Frances Elizabeth Cox ('Jesus lives!') and Catherine Winkworth ('Now thank we all our God'). These two were among many gifted women writers of the time, including Cecil Frances Alexander ('All things bright and beautiful', 'Once in royal David's city', 'There is a green hill far away') and Christina Rossetti, whose 'In the bleak mid-winter' is as clear and sharp as a medieval manuscript illumination.

Two American hymns were included in the first edition of *Hymns Ancient and Modern*, and the energetic growth of American hymnody in the nineteenth century paralleled that of English. 'It came upon the midnight clear' is an eloquent prayer for peace, written not long before the Civil War, and Julia Ward Howe's 'Battle Hymn of the Republic' was written during that war, after seeing a troop review. More peacefully, Phillips Brooks reconstructs the scene of the dark streets of Bethlehem in 'O little town' with a magical repetition:

> How silently, how silently,
>   The wondrous gift is given . . .

By the end of the nineteenth century, on both sides of the Atlantic, the trickle of hymns had become a flood, posing problems for the editors of hymn-books. *The English Hymnal* (1906) and *Songs of Praise* (1926), the two most original hymn-books of the twentieth century, unearthed even more treasures, such as 'Drop, drop, slow tears' and 'Morning has broken'; while the music, edited principally by Vaughan Williams, replaced many of the Victorian tunes with fresh English folk music.

So the hymn lover of today has a rich heritage from which to choose. Those hymns which have stood the test of time are those which express the deepest thoughts of the human heart with honesty and sympathy, and which follow the gospel message with fidelity and integrity. They do so in verse which comforts through its familiarity and inspires through its poetry. Other elements in worship are vital, such as prayer and preaching – and hymns also pray and teach. Compared with prayer and preaching, however, the finest hymns have something else – a force, a beauty, a grace – which makes them beloved and special, so that, in the words of Herbert,

> A verse may find him, who a sermon flies,
> And turn delight into a sacrifice.
>
> (*George Herbert,* 'The Church-porch')

RICHARD WATSON
Professor of English
University of Durham

TRADITIONAL
HYMNS

MORNING

AWAKE, MY SOUL, AND WITH THE SUN

F. H. BARTHÉLÉMON, 1741-1808

AWAKE, my soul, and with the sun
Thy daily stage of duty run;
Shake off dull sloth, and joyful rise
To pay thy morning sacrifice.

2 Redeem thy mis-spent time that's past;
Live this day as if 'twere thy last;
Improve thy talent with due care;
For the great day thyself prepare.

3 Let all thy converse be sincere,
Thy conscience as the noon-day clear;
Think how all-seeing God thy ways
And all thy secret thoughts surveys.

4 By influence of the Light divine
Let thy own light in good works shine;
Reflect all heaven's propitious ways
In ardent love and cheerful praise.

5 Wake, and lift up thyself, my heart,
And with the angels bear thy part,
Who all night long unwearied sing
High praise to the eternal King.

6 Awake, awake, ye heavenly choir,
May your devotion me inspire,
That I like you my age may spend,
Like you may on my God attend.

7   Glory to thee, who safe hast kept
    And hast refreshed me whilst I slept;
    Grant, Lord, when I from death shall wake
    I may of endless light partake.

8   Heaven is, dear Lord, where'er thou art,
    O never then from me depart;
    For to my soul 'tis hell to be
    But for one moment void of thee.

9   Lord, I my vows to thee renew;
    Scatter my sins as morning dew;
    Guard my first springs of thought and will,
    And with thyself my spirit fill.

10 Direct, control, suggest, this day
    All I design, or do, or say;
    That all my powers, with all their might,
    In thy sole glory may unit.

Doxology after any Part

11 Praise God, from whom all blessings flow;
    Praise him, all creatures here below;
    Praise him above, ye heavenly host;
    Praise Father, Son, and Holy Ghost.

Bishop T. Ken, 1637-1711

MORNING HAS BROKEN

Old Gaelic Melody

MORNING has broken
Like the first morning,
Blackbird has spoken
Like the first bird.
Praise for the singing!
Praise for the morning!
Praise for them, springing
Fresh from the Word!

2 Sweet the rain's new fall
Sunlit from heaven,
Like the first dewfall
On the first grass.
Praise for the sweetness
Of the wet garden,
Sprung in completeness
Where his feet pass.

3 Mine is the sunlight!
Mine is the morning
Born of the one light
Eden saw play!
Praise with elation,
Praise every morning,
God's re-creation
Of the new day!

Eleanor Farjeon, 1881-1965

EVENING

Abide with me

W. H. MONK, 1823-89

ABIDE with me; fast falls the eventide;
The darkness deepens; Lord, with me abide!
When other helpers fail, and comforts flee,
Help of the helpless, O abide with me.

2 Swift to its close ebbs out life's little day;
Earth's joys grow dim, its glories pass away;
Change and decay in all around I see;
O though who changest not, abide with me.

3 I need thy presence every passing hour;
What but thy grace can foil the tempter's power?
Who like thyself my guide and stay can be?
Through cloud and sunshine, O abide with me.

4 I fear no foe with thee at hand to bless;
Ills have no weight, and tears no bitterness.
Where is death's sting? Where, grave, thy victory?
I triumph still, if thou abide with me.

5 Hold thou thy cross before my closing eyes;
    Shine through the gloom, and point me to the skies;
    Heaven's morning breaks, and earth's vain shadows flee;
    In life, in death, O Lord, abide with me!

        H. F. *Lyte*, 1793-1847

NOW THE DAY IS OVER

S. BARING-GOULD, 1834-1924

NOW the day is over,
   Night is drawing nigh,
Shadows of the evening
   Steal across the sky.

2 Now the darkness gathers,
   Stars begin to peep,
Birds and beasts and flowers
   Soon will be asleep.

3 Jesus, give the weary
   Calm and sweet repose;
With thy tenderest blessing
   May our eyelids close.

4 Grant to little children
   Visions bright of thee;
Guard the sailors tossing
   On the deep blue sea.

5 Comfort every sufferer
   Watching late in pain;
Those who plan some evil
   From their sin restrain.

6 Through the long night watches
   May thine angels spread
Their white wings above me,
   Watching round my bed.

7 When the morning wakens,
   Then may I arise
Pure, and fresh, and sinless
   In thy holy eyes.

8 Glory to the Father,
   Glory to the Son,
And to thee, blest Spirit,
   Whilst all ages run.

S. Baring-Gould, 1834-1924

THE DAY THOU GAVEST, LORD, IS ENDED

Composed or adapted by L. BOURGEOIS
for the *Genevan Psalter*, 1543

THE day thou gavest, Lord, is ended,
　　The darkness falls at thy behest;
To thee our morning hymns ascended,
　　Thy praise shall sanctify our rest.

2　We thank thee that thy Church un-sleeping,
　　　While earth rolls onward into light,
　　Through all the world her watch is keeping,
　　　And rests not now by day or night.

3　As o'er each continent and island
　　　The dawn leads on another day,
　　The voice of prayer is never silent,
　　　Nor dies the strain of praise away.

4　The sun that bids us rest is waking
　　　Our brethren 'neath the western sky,
　　And hour by hour fresh lips are making
　　　Thy wondrous doings heard on high.

5 So be it, Lord; thy throne shall never,
    Like earth's proud empires, pass away;
  Thy kingdom stands, and grows for ever,
    Till all thy creatures own thy sway.

J. Ellerton, 1826-93

Evening

GLORY TO THEE, MY GOD, THIS NIGHT

T. TALLIS, c. 1510-85

GLORY to thee, my God, this night
For all the blessings of the light;
Keep me, O keep me, King of Kings,
Beneath thy own almighty wings.

2   Forgive me, Lord, for thy dear Son,
    The ill that I this day have done,
    That with the world, myself, and thee,
    I, ere I sleep, at peace may be.

3   Teach me to live, that I may dread
    The grave as little as my bed;
    Teach me to die, that so I may
    Rise glorious at the aweful day.

4   O may my soul on thee repose,
    And with sweet sleep mine eyelids close,
    Sleep that may me more vigorous make
    To serve my God when I awake.

5   Praise God, from whom all blessings flow;
    Praise him, all creatures here below;
    Praise him above, ye heavenly host;
    Praise Father, Son, and Holy Ghost.

26   *Bishop T. Ken, 1637-1711*

GOD, THAT MADEST EARTH AND HEAVEN

Welsh Traditional Melody

GOD, that madest earth and heaven,
    Darkness and light;
Who the day for toil hast given,
    For rest the night;
May thine angel-guards defend us,
Slumber sweet thy mercy send us,
Holy dreams and hopes attend us,
    This livelong night.

2 Guard us waking, guard us sleeping;
    And, when we die,
May we in thy mighty keeping
    All peaceful lie:
So when death to life shall wake us,
Thou may'st like the angels make us,
And to reign in glory take us
    With thee on high.

1. Bishop Heber(1827) *2. Archbishop Whately* (1855)

O GLADSOME LIGHT

Composed or adapted by L. BOURGEOIS, in 1549, for the
Genevan Psalter. Harmony chiefly from C. Goudimel (d. 1572)

O GLADSOME light, O grace
Of God the Father's face,
The eternal splendour wearing;
Celestial, holy, blest,
Our Saviour Jesus Christ,
Joyful in thine appearing.

2 Now, ere day fadeth quite,
   We see the evening light,
Our wonted hymn outpouring;
Father of might unknown,
Thee, his incarnate Son,
And Holy Spirit adoring.

3 To thee of right belongs
   All praise of holy songs,
O Son of God, lifegiver;
   Thee, therefore, O most high,
   The world doth glorify,
And shalt exalt for ever.

R. Bridges, 1844-1930, based on 7th-century hymn.

HARVEST

LET US, WITH A GLADSOME MIND

Melody from *Hymn Tunes of the United Brethren*, 1824.
Arranged by J. WILKES (1861)

LET US, with a gladsome mind,
Praise the Lord, for he is kind:

> *For his mercies ay endure,*
> *Ever faithful, ever sure.*

2 Let us blaze his name abroad,
For of gods he is the God:

3 He with all-commanding might
Filled the new-made world with light:

4 He the golden-tressèd sun
Caused all day his course to run:

5 The hornèd moon to shine by night,
'Mid her spangled sisters bright:

6 All things living he doth feed,
His full hand supplies their need:

7 Let us, with a gladsome mind,
Praise the Lord, for he is kind:

J. Milton, 1608-74

31

WE PLOUGH THE FIELDS, AND SCATTER

Bible Class Magazine, 1854, said to be arranged from
J.A. P. SCHULZ, 1747-1800

WE plough the fields, and scatter
⠀⠀⠀The good seed on the land,
But it is fed and watered
⠀⠀By God's almighty hand:
He sends the snow in winter,
⠀⠀The warmth to swell the grain,
The breezes and the sunshine,
⠀⠀And soft refreshing rain:

⠀⠀⠀*All good gifts around us*
⠀⠀⠀⠀*Are sent from heaven above;*
⠀⠀⠀*Then thank the Lord, O thank the Lord,*
⠀⠀⠀⠀*For all his love.*

2⠀He only is the maker
⠀⠀⠀Of all things near and far,
⠀⠀He paints the wayside flower,
⠀⠀⠀He lights the evening star.
⠀⠀The winds and waves obey him,
⠀⠀⠀By him the birds are fed;
⠀⠀Much more to us, his children,
⠀⠀⠀He gives our daily bread:

3⠀We thank thee then, O Father,
⠀⠀⠀For all things bright and good;
⠀⠀The seed-time and the harvest,
⠀⠀⠀Our life, our health, our food.
⠀⠀No gifts have we to offer
⠀⠀⠀For all thy love imparts,
⠀⠀But that which thou desirest,
⠀⠀⠀Our humble, thankful hearts:

M. *Claudius*, 1740-1815. *Tr. J. M. Campbell.*

ADVENT

Lo! HE COMES WITH CLOUDS DESCENDING

English Melody of the 18th century

L O! he comes with clouds descending,
   Once for favoured sinners slain;
Thousand thousand saints attending
   Swell the triumph of his train:
     Alleluya!
   God appears, on earth to reign.

2 Every eye shall now behold him
   Robed in glorious majesty;
Those who set at nought and sold him,
   Pierced and nailed him to the tree,
     Deeply wailing,
   Shall their true Messiah see.

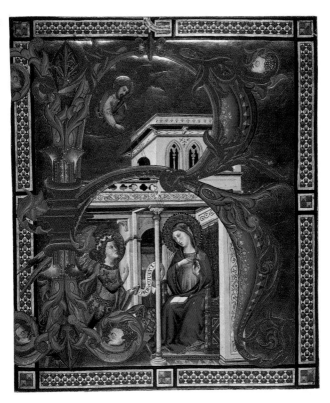

3 Those dear tokens of his passion
  Still his dazzling body bears;
  Cause of wondering exultation
   To his countless worshippers;
    With what rapture
   Praise we him for all his scars!

4 Yea, amen, let all adore thee,
  High on thine eternal throne;
  Saviour, take the power and glory:
   Claim the kingdom as thine own:
    Alleluya!
   Thou shalt reign, and thou alone.

C. Wesley (1758), *and others*   37

O COME, O COME, EMMANUEL

Adapted by T. HELMORE, 1811-90,

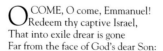

O COME, O come, Emmanuel!
Redeem thy captive Israel,
That into exile drear is gone
Far from the face of God's dear Son:

Rejoice! Rejoice! Emmanuel
Shall come to thee, O Israel.

2 O come, thou Branch of Jesse! draw
   The quarry from the lion's claw
   From the dread caverns of the grave,
   From nether hell, thy people save:

3 O come, O come, thou Dayspring bright!
   Pour on our souls thy healing light;
   Dispel the long night's lingering gloom,
   And pierce the shadows of the tomb:

4 O come, thou Lord of David's key!
   The royal door fling wide and free;
   Safeguard for us the heavenward road,
   And bar the way to death's abode:

5 O come, O come, Adonaï,
   Who in thy glorious majesty
   From that high mountain clothed with awe
   Gavest thy folk the elder law:

18th cent. Tr. T. A. Lacey

39

Hark! a herald voice is calling

W. H. MONK, 1823-89

Hark! a herald voice is calling:
    'Christ is nigh,' it seems to say;
'Cast away the dreams of darkness,
    O ye children of the day!'

2 Wakened by the solemn warning,
    Let the earth-bound soul arise;
Christ, her Sun, all sloth dispelling,
    Shines upon the morning skies.

3 Lo! the Power, so long expected,
    Comes with pardon down from heaven;
Let us haste, with tears of sorrow,
    One and all to be forgiven;

4 So when love comes forth in judgment,
    Debts and doubts and wrongs to clear,
Faithful may he find his servants,
    Watching till the dawn appear.

5 Honour, glory, might, and blessing
    To the Father and the Son
And the eternal Spirit give we,
    While unending ages run.

6th cent. S. P. V.

Hark the glad sound

Melody from *Ravenscroft's Psalter*, 1621

Hark the glad sound! the Saviour comes,
  The Saviour promised long!
Let every heart prepare a throne,
  And every voice a song.

2 He comes the prisoners to release
    In Satan's bondage held;
  The gates of brass before him burst,
    The iron fetters yield.

3 He comes the broken heart to bind,
    The bleeding soul to cure,
  And with the treasures of his grace
    To enrich the humble poor.

4 Our glad hosannas, Prince of peace,
    Thy welcome shall proclaim;
  And heaven's eternal arches ring
    With thy belovèd name.

P. Doddridge, 1702-51

HILLS OF THE NORTH, REJOICE

MARTIN SHAW, 1875-1958

HILLS of the North, rejoice;
    River and mountain-spring,
Hark to the advent voice;
    Valley and lowland, sing;
Though absent long, your Lord is nigh;
He judgment brings and victory.

2 Isles of the southern seas,
    Deep in your coral caves
    Pent be each warring breeze,
    Lulled be your restless waves:
He comes to reign with boundless sway,
And makes your wastes his great highway.

3 Lands of the East, awake,
    Soon shall your sons be free;
    The sleep of ages break,
    And rise to liberty.
On your far hills, long cold and grey,
Has dawned the everlasting day.

4 Shores of the utmost West,
      Ye that have waited long,
         Unvisited, unblest,
      Break forth to swelling song;
   High raise the note, that Jesus died,
   Yet lives and reigns, the Crucified.

5 Shout, while ye journey home;
      Songs be in every mouth;
         Lo, from the North we come,
      From East, and West, and South.
   City of God, the bond are free,
   We come to live and reign in thee!

   Charles E. Oakley, 1832-65

43

✠

✠

CHRISTMAS

A GREAT AND MIGHTY WONDER

Old German Melody, harmony by M. PRAETORIUS, 1571-1621

A GREAT and mighty wonder,
A full and blessed cure!
The Rose has come to blossom
Which shall for ay endure:

Repeat the hymn again!
'To God on high be glory,
And peace on earth to men.'

2 The Word has dwelt among us,
The true light from on high;
And cherubim sing anthems
To shepherds, from the sky:

3 While thus they sing your
Monarch,
Those bright angelic bands,
Rejoice, ye vales and mountains,
Ye oceans, clap your hands:

4 Since all he comes to succour,
By all be he adored,
The infant born in Bethlem,
The Saviour and the Lord:

5 And idol forms shall perish,
And error shall decay,
And Christ shall wield his sceptre,
Our Lord and God for ay:

46   *St. Germanus, 634-734. Tr. J. M. Neale*

IT CAME UPON THE MIDNIGHT CLEAR

Traditional Air, adapted by A. SULLIVAN, 1842-1900

IT came upon the midnight clear,
    That glorious song of old,
From angels bending near the earth
    To touch their harps of gold:
'Peace on the earth, good will to men,
    From heaven's all-gracious King!'
The World in solemn stillness lay
    To hear the angels sing.

2 Still through the cloven skies they come,
    With peaceful wings unfurled;
And still their heavenly music floats
    O'er all the weary world;
Above its sad and lowly plains
    They bend on hovering wing;
And ever o'er its Babel sounds
    The blessèd angels sing.

3 Yet with the woes of sin and strife
    The world has suffered long;
Beneath the angel-strain have rolled
    Two thousand years of wrong;
And man, at war with man, hears not
    The love-song which they bring:
O hush the noise, ye men of strife,
    And hear the angels sing.

4 And ye, beneath life's crushing load,
    Whose forms are bending low,
Who toil along the climbing way
    With painful steps and slow,
Look now! for glad and golden hours
    Come swiftly on the wing;
O rest beside the weary road,
    And hear the angels sing.

5 For lo! the days are hastening on,
    By prophet-bards foretold,
When, with the ever-circling years,
    Comes round the age of gold;
When peace shall over all the earth
    Its ancient splendours fling,
And the whole world give back the song
    Which now the angels sing.

E. H. Sears, 1810-76

O LITTLE TOWN OF BETHLEHEM

English Traditional Melody

O LITTLE town of Bethlehem,
   How still we see thee lie!
Above thy deep and dreamless sleep
   The silent stars go by.
Yet in thy dark streets shineth
   The everlasting light;
The hopes and fears of all the years
   Are met in thee to-night.

2 O morning stars, together
   Proclaim the holy birth,
And praises sing to God the King,
   And peace to men on earth;
For Christ is born of Mary;
   And, gathered all above,
While mortals sleep, the angels kee
   Their watch of wondering love.

3 How silently, how silently,
   The wondrous gift is given!
So God imparts to human hearts
   The blessings of his heaven.
No ear may hear his coming;
   But in this world of sin,
Where meek souls will receive him, still
   The dear Christ enters in.

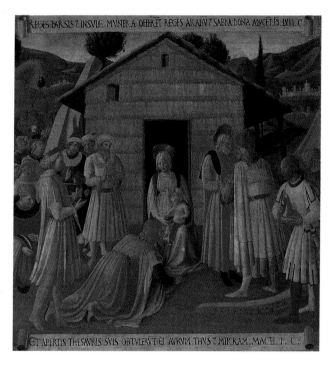

REGES THARSIS Z INSVLE MVNER A OFFERET REGES ARABV Z SABBA DONA ADVCET.PS.LXXI.C

ET APERTIS THESAVRIS SVIS OBTVLERVT EI AVRVM THVS Z MIR.RAM.MACEL. I. C

Where children pure and happy
    Pray to the blessèd child,
Where misery cries out to thee,
    Son of the mother mild;
Where charity stands watching
    And faith holds wide the door,
The dark night wakes, the glory breaks,
    And Christmas comes once more.

5 O holy Child of Bethlehem,
    Descend to us, we pray;
Cast out our sin, and enter in,
    Be born in us to-day.
We hear the Christmas angels
    The great glad tidings tell:
O come to us, abide with us,
    Our Lord Emmanuel.

Bp. Phillips Brooks, 1835-93

ANGELS, FROM THE REALMS OF GLORY

French Carol Melody

ANGELS, from the realms of glory,
    Wing your flight o'er all the earth;
Ye who sang creation's story
    Now proclaim Messiah's birth:

Come and worship,
Worship Christ, the new-born King.

2 Shepherds in the fields abiding,
    Watching o'er your flocks by night,
God with man is now residing;
    Yonder shines the infant Light:

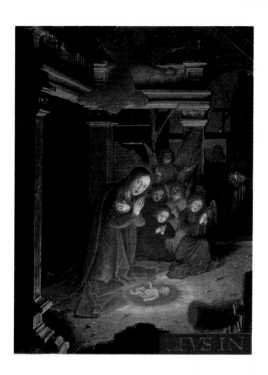

3 Sages, leave your contemplations;
      Brighter visions beam afar;
   Seek the great Desire of Nations;
      Ye have seen his natal star:

4 Saints before the altar bending,
      Watching long in hope and fear,
   Suddenly the Lord, descending,
      In his temple shall appear:

5 Though an infant now we view him,
      He shall fill his Father's throne,
   Gather all the nations to him;
      Every knee shall then bow down:

J. Montgomery, 1771-1854

Unto us a boy is born!

From *Piae Cantiones*, 1582
Arranged by GEOFFREY SHAW, 1879-1943

UNTO us a boy is born!
  King of all creation,
Came he to a world forlorn,
  The Lord of every nation.

2 Cradled in a stall was he
     With sleepy cows and asses;
   But the very beasts could see
     That he all men surpasses.

3 Herod then with fear was filled:
     'A prince', he said, 'in Jewry!'
   All the little boys he killed
     At Bethlem in his fury.

4 Now may Mary's son, who came
     So long ago to love us,
   Lead us all with hearts aflame
     Unto the joys above us.

5 He the Source and he the End!
     Let the organ thunder,
   While our happy voices rend
     The jocund air asunder!

15th-century Carol

WHILE SHEPHERDS WATCHED THEIR FLOCKS BY NIGHT

First appeared in *Este's Psalter*, 1592

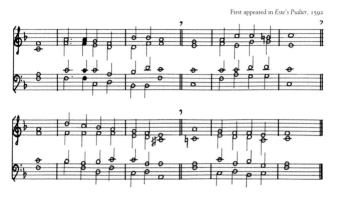

WHILE shepherds watched their flocks by night,
    All seated on the ground,
The angel of the Lord came down,
    And glory shone around.

2 'Fear not,' said he (for mighty dread
    Had seized their troubled mind);
'Glad tidings of great joy I bring
    To you and all mankind.

3 'To you in David's town this day
    Is born of David's line
A saviour, who is Christ the Lord;
    And this shall be the sign:

4 'The heavenly babe you there shall find
    To human view displayed,
All meanly wrapped in swathing bands
    And in a manger laid.'

5 Thus spake the seraph; and forthwith
    Appeared a shining throng
Of angels praising God, who thus
    Addressed their joyful song:

6 'All glory be to God on high,
    And to the earth be peace;
Good will henceforth from heaven to men
    Begin and never cease.'

Nahum Tate, 1652-1715

55

CHRISTIANS, AWAKE, SALUTE THE HAPPY MORN

J. WAINWRIGHT, 1723-68

CHRISTIANS, awake, salute the happy morn,
Whereon the Saviour of the World was born;
Rise to adore the mystery of love,
Which hosts of angels chanted from above;
With them the joyful tidings first begun
Of God incarnate and the Virgin's Son.

56

2 Then to the watchful shepherds it was told,
   Who heard the angelic herald's voice, 'Behold,
   I bring good tidings of a saviour's birth
   To you and all the nations upon earth;
   This day hath God fulfilled his promised word,
   This day is born a saviour, Christ the Lord.'

3 He spake; and straightway the celestial choir
   In hymns of joy, unknown before, conspire.
   The praises of redeeming love they sang,
   And heaven's whole orb with alleluyas rang:
   God's highest glory was their anthem still,
   Peace upon earth, and unto men good will.

4 To Bethlehem straight the enlightened shepherds ran,
   To see the wonder God had wrought for man.
   He that was born upon this joyful day
   Around us all his glory shall display:
   Saved by his love, incessant we shall sing
   Eternal praise to heaven's almighty King.

John Byrom, 1692-1763

Christmas

Away in a Manger

Melody by W. J. KIRKPATRICK, 1838-1921

AWAY in a manger, no crib for a bed,
The little Lord Jesus laid down his sweet head.
The stars in the bright sky looked down where he lay,
The little Lord Jesus asleep on the hay.

2 The cattle are lowing, the baby awakes,
But little Lord Jesus no crying he makes.
I love thee, Lord Jesus! Look down from the sky,
And stay by my bedside till morning is nigh.

3 Be near me, Lord Jesus; I ask thee to stay
Close by me for ever, and love me, I pray.
Bless all the dear children in thy tender care,
And fit us for heaven, to live with thee there.

Anon.

O COME, ALL YE FAITHFUL

J. WADE, *c.* 1711-86

O COME, all ye faithful,
  Joyful and triumphant,
O come ye, O come ye to Bethlehem;
  Come and behold him,
  Born the King of angels:

  O come, let us adore him,
  O come, let us adore him,
  O come, let us adore him, Christ the Lord!

2 God of God,
   Light of Light,
Lo, he abhors not the Virgin's womb;
   Very God,
   Begotten, not created:

3 See how the shepherds,
   Summonded to his cradle,
Leaving their flocks, draw nigh to gaze;
   We too will thither
   Bend our joyful footsteps:

4 Lo, star-led chieftains,
   Magi, Christ adoring,
Offer him incense, gold, and myrrh;
   We to the Christ-child
   Bring our hearts' oblations:

5 Child, for us sinners
   Poor and in the manger,
Fain we embrace thee, with love and awe;
   Who would not love thee,
   Loving us so dearly?

6 Sing, choirs of angels,
   Sing in exultation,
Sing, all ye citizens of heaven above;
   Glory to God
   In the highest:

(Christmas Day only.)

7 Yea, Lord, we greet thee,
   Born this happy morning,
Jesus, to thee be glory given;
   Word of the Father,
   Now in flesh appearing:

J. Wade, c. 1711-86.
Tr. F. Oakeley, and others.

ONCE IN ROYAL DAVID'S CITY

H. J. GAUNTLETT, 1805-76

ONCE in royal David's city
    Stood a lowly cattle shed,
Where a mother laid her baby
    In a manger for his bed:
Mary was that mother mild,
Jesus Christ her little child.

2 He came down to earth from heaven,
        Who is God and Lord of all,
    And his shelter was a stable,
        And his cradle was a stall;
    With the poor, and mean, and lowly,
    Lived on earth our Saviour holy.

62

3 And through all his wondrous childhood
    He would honour and obey,
Love and watch the lowly maiden,
    In whose gentle arms he lay:
Christian children all must be
Mild, obedient, good as he.

4 For he is our childhood's pattern:
    Day by day like us he grew,
He was little, weak, and helpless,
    Tears and smiles like us he knew;
And he feeleth for our sadness,
And he shareth in our gladness.

5 And our eyes at last shall see him,
    Through his own redeeming love,
For that child so dear and gentle
    Is our Lord in heaven above;
And he leads his children on
To the place where he is gone.

Mrs C. F. Alexander, 1818-95

HARK! THE HERALD ANGELS SING

Adapted from a Chorus by F. MENDELSSOHN-BARTHOLDY, 1809-47

HARK! the herald angels sing
Glory to the new-born King;
Peace on earth and mercy mild,
God and sinners reconciled:
Joyful all ye nations rise,
Join the triumph of the skies,
With the angelic host proclaim,
Christ is born in Bethlehem:

> *Hark! the herald angels sing*
> *Glory to the new-born King.*

2 Christ, by highest heaven adored,
   Christ, the everlasting Lord,
   Late in time behold him come
   Offspring of the Virgin's womb;
   Veiled in flesh the Godhead see;
   Hail the incarnate Deity!
   Pleased as man with man to dwell,
   Jesus, our Emmanuel:

3 Hail the heaven-born Prince of Peace!
   Hail the Sun of Righteousness!
   Light and life to all he brings,
   Risen with healing in his wings;
   Mild he lays his glory by,
   Born that man no more may die,
   Born to raise the sons of earth,
   Born to give them second birth:

C. *Wesley* (1743), G. *Whitefield* (1753),
   M.*Madan* (1760), *and others*

THE FIRST NOEL

English Traditional Carol Melody

THE first Noel the angel did say
Was to certain poor shepherds in fields as they lay;
In fields where they lay, keeping their sheep,
In a cold winter's night that was so deep:

Noel, noel, noel, noel,
Born is the King of Israel!

2 Then wise men, guided by a star,
Came from the eastern countries far;
To seek for a king was their intent,
And to follow the star wheresoever it went:

3 This star drew nigh to the north-west;
   O'er Bethlehem it took its rest,
   And there it did both stop and stay
   Right over the place where Jesus lay:

MARY HAD A BABY

West Indian Spiritual

MARY had a baby, yes, Lord,
Mary had a baby, yes, my Lord,
Mary had a baby, yes, Lord!
The people keep a-coming, but the train has gone!

2 What did she name him, yes Lord,
   what did she name him, yes my Lord,
   what did she name him, yes, Lord?
   The people keep a-coming, but the train has gone!

3 Mary named him Jesus, yes, Lord,
   Mary named him Jesus, yes, my Lord,
   Mary named him Jesus, yes, Lord!
   The people keep a-coming, but the train has gone!

68

4 Where was he born, yes, Lord,
   where was he born, yes, my Lord,
   where was he born, yes, Lord?
   The people keep a-coming, but the train has gone!

5 Born in a stable, yes, Lord,
   born in a stable, yes, my Lord,
   born in a stable, yes, Lord?
   The people keep a-coming, but the train has gone!

6 Where did she lay him, yes, Lord,
   where did she lay him, yes, my Lord,
   where did she lay him, yes, Lord?
   The people keep a-coming, but the train has gone!

7 Laid him in a manger, yes, Lord,
   laid him in a manger, yes, my Lord,
   laid him in a manger, yes, Lord!
   The people keep a-coming, but the train has gone!

69

IN THE BLEAK MID-WINTER

GUSTAV HOLST, 1874-1934

Verses 2-3

IN the bleak mid-winter
  Frosty wind made moan;
Earth stood hard as iron,
  Water like a stone;
Snow had fallen, snow on snow,
  Snow on snow,
In the bleak mid-winter,
  Long ago.

2 Our God, heaven cannot hold him
    Nor earth sustain;
  Heaven and earth shall flee away
    When he comes to reign:
  In the bleak mid-winter
    A stable-place sufficed
  The Lord God almighty,
    Jesus Christ.

3 Enough for him, whom cherubim
    Worship night and day,
  A breastful of milk,
    And a mangerful of hay;
  Enough for him, whom angels
    Fall down before,
  The ox and ass and camel
    Which adore.

4 Angels and archangels
    May have gathered there,
  Cherubim and seraphim
    Thronged the air:
  But only his mother
    In her maiden bliss
  Worshipped the Belovèd
    With a kiss.

5 What can I give him,
    Poor as I am?
  If I were a shepherd
    I would bring a lamb;
  If I were a wise man
    I would do my part;
  Yet what I can I give him –
    Give my heart.

Christina Rossetti, 1830-94

✠

✠

EPIPHANY

AS WITH GLADNESS MEN OF OLD

Abridged from a Chorale, 'Treuer Heiland', by C. KOCHER, 1786-1872

AS with gladness men of old
Did the guiding star behold,
As with joy they hailed its light,
Leading onward, beaming bright,
So, most gracious God, may we
Evermore be led to thee.

2 As with joyful steps they sped
   To that lowly manger-bed,
   There to bend the knee before
   Him whom heaven and earth adore,
   So may we with willing feet
   Ever seek thy mercy-seat.

3 As they offered gifts most rare
   At that manger rude and bare,
   So may we with holy joy,
   Pure, and free from sin's alloy,
   All our costliest treasures bring,
   Christ, to thee our heavenly King.

4 Holy Jesus, every day
 Keep us in the narrow way;
 And, when earthly things are past,
 Bring our ransomed souls at last
 Where they need no star to guide,
 Where no clouds thy glory hide.

5 In the heavenly country bright
 Need they no created light;
 Thou its light, its joy, its crown,
 Thou its sun which goes not down:
 There for ever may we sing
 Alleluyas to our King.

W. Chatterton Dix, 1837-98

BRIGHTEST AND BEST OF THE SONS OF THE MORNING

Later form of melody from *Himmels-Lust*, 1679

BRIGHTEST and best of the sons of the morning,
  Dawn on our darkness and lend us thine aid;
Star of the east, the horizon adorning,
  Guide where our infant Redeemer is laid.

2 Cold on his cradle the dew-drops are shining,
    Low lies his head with the beasts of the stall:
Angels adore him in slumber reclining,
    Maker and monarch and saviour of all.

3 Say, shall we yield him, in costly devotion,
    Odours of Edom and offerings divine?
Gems of the mountain and pearls of the ocean,
    Myrrh from the forest or gold from the mine?

4 Vainly we offer each ample oblation,
    Vainly with gifts would his favour secure;
Richer by far is the heart's adoration,
    Dearer to God are the prayers of the poor.

5 Brightest and best of the sons of the morning,
    Dawn on our darkness and lend us thine aid;
Star of the east, the horizon adorning,
    Guide where our infant Redeemer is laid.

Bishop R. Heber, 1783-1826

HOW BRIGHTLY BEAMS THE MORNING STAR!

Later form of melody by P. NICOLAI (1556-1608). Harmonized by
J. S. BACH, 1685-1750

HOW brightly beams the morning star!
What sudden radiance from afar
   Doth glad us with its shining?
Brightness of God, that breaks our night
And fills the darkened souls with light
   Who long for truth were pining!
     Newly, truly, God's word feeds us,
       Rightly leads us,
        Life bestowing.
Praise, O praise such love o'erflowing!

2 Through thee alone can we be blest;
  Then deep be on our hearts imprest
    The love that thou hast borne us;
  So make us ready to fulfil
  With ardent zeal thy holy will,
    Though men may vex or scorn us;
  Hold us, fold us, lest we fail thee.

      Lo, we hail thee,
      Long to know thee!
  All we are and have we owe thee.

3 All praise to him who came to save,
  Who conquer'd death and scorned the grave;
    Each day new praise resoundeth
  To him, the Life who once was slain,
  The friend whom none shall trust in vain,
    Whose grace for ay aboundeth;
  Sing then, ring then, tell the story
      Of his glory,
      Till his praises
  Flood with light earth's darkest mazes!

P. Nicolai (1599) *and J. A. Schlegel* (1766)

BETHLEHEM, OF NOBLEST CITIES

Adapted from a melody in Psalmodia Sacra, Gotha, 1715

BETHLEHEM, of noblest cities
None can once with thee compare;
Thou alone the Lord from heaven
Didst for us incarnate bear.

2 Fairer than the sun at morning
Was the star that told his birth;
To the lands their God announcing,
Hid beneath a form of earth.

3 By its lambent beauty guided
See the eastern kings appear;
See them bend, their gifts to offer,
Gifts of incense, gold, and myrrh.

4 Solemn things of mystic meaning:
Incense doth the God disclose,
Gold a royal child proclaimeth,
Myrrh a future tomb foreshows.

5 Holy Jesus, in thy brightness
To the Gentile world displayed,
With the Father and the Spirit
Endless praise to thee be paid

Prudentius, b. 348. Tr. E. Caswall

LENT

Aʜ, ʜᴏʟʏ Jᴇsᴜs

Later form of melody by J. CRÜGER, 1598-1662

Aʜ, holy Jesus, how hast thou offended,
That man to judge thee hath in hate pretended?
By foes derided, by thine own rejected,
O most afflicted.

2 Who was the guilty? Who brought this upon thee?
Alas, my treason, Jesus, hath undone thee.
'Twas I, Lord Jesus, I it was denied thee:
I crucified thee.

3 Lo, the good Shepherd for the sheep is offered;
The slave hath sinnèd, and the Son hath suffered;
For man's atonement, while he nothing heedeth,
God intercedeth.

4 For me, kind Jesus, was thy incarnation,
Thy mortal sorrow, and thy life's oblation;
Thy death of anguish and thy bitter passion,
For my salvation.

PERCVTIENT MAXILLAM IVDICIS ISRL. MICHEE . V . C

ASSISTES MINISTRORV DEDIT ALAPA VHM DICES SIC REPODES PONTIFICI IO XVIII

5 Therefore, kind Jesus, since I cannot pay thee,
   I do adore thee, and will ever pray thee,
      Think on thy pity and thy love unswerving,
         Not my deserving.

J. Heermann, 1585-1647. Tr. R. Bridges   83

Lord Jesus, Think on Me

Damon's Psalter, 1579

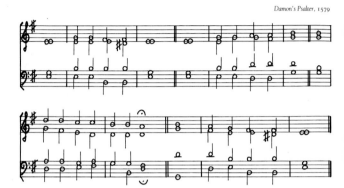

L ORD Jesus, think on me
  And purge away my sin;
From earthborn passions set me free,
  And make me pure within.

2 Lord Jesus, think on me,
    With care and woe opprest;
  Let me thy loving servant be,
    And taste thy promised rest.

3 Lord Jesus, think on me
    Amid the battle's strife;
  In all my pain and misery
    Be thou my health and life.

4 Lord Jesus, think on me,
    Nor let me go astray;
  Through darkness and perplexity
    Point thou the heavenly way.

5 Lord Jesus, think on me
    When flows the tempest high:
  When on doth rush the enemy,
    O Saviour, be thou nigh.

6 Lord Jesus, think on me,
    That, when the flood is past,
  I may the eternal brightness see,
    And share thy joy at last.

Bp. Synesius, 375-430. Tr. A. W. Chatfield

Forty days and forty nights

Probably by MARTIN HERBST, 1654-81

Forty days and forty nights
Thou wast fasting in the wild;
Forty days and forty nights
Tempted still, yet unbeguiled:

2 Sunbeams scorching all the day,
Chilly dew-drops nightly shed,
Prowling beasts about thy way,
Stones thy pillow, earth thy bed.

3 Let us thy endurance share
And from earthly greed abstain,
With thee watching unto prayer,
With thee strong to suffer pain.

4 Then if evil on us press,
Flesh or spirit to assail,
Victor in the wilderness,
Help us not to swerve or fail!

5 So shall peace divine be ours;
Holier gladness ours shall be;
Come to us angelic powers,
Such as ministered to thee.

6 Keep, O keep us, Saviour dear,
Ever constant by thy side,
That with thee we may appear
At the eternal Eastertide.

G. H. Smyttan, 1822-70, and others

Be thou my guardian

I. SMITH, c. 1725-c. 1800

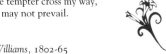

BE thou my guardian and my guide,
　　And hear me when I call;
Let not my slippery footsteps slide,
　　And hold me lest I fall.

2　The world, the flesh, and Satan dwell
　　　Around the path I tread;
　　O save me from the snares of hell,
　　　Thou quickener of the dead.

3　And if I tempted am to sin,
　　　And outward things are strong,
　　Do thou, O Lord, keep watch within,
　　　And save my soul from wrong.

4　Still let me ever watch and pray,
　　　And feel that I am frail;
　　That if the tempter cross my way,
　　　Yet he may not prevail.

86　　　　　　*I. Williams, 1802-65*

QVI EDEBAT PANES MEOS MAGNIFICAVIT SVP ME SVPPLATATOEM . PS . XL.

ET COFESTIM ACCEDES IVDAS AD XPM DIXIT AVE RABBI. OSTVLATVS E. EV. MXXVI

87

O FOR A CLOSER WALK WITH GOD

Melody in *Scottish Psalter*, 1635

O FOR a closer walk with God,
    A calm and heavenly frame;
A light to shine upon the road
    That leads me to the Lamb!

2 Return, O holy Dove, return,
       Sweet messenger of rest;
    I hate the sins that made thee mourn,
       And drove thee from my breast.

3 The dearest idol I have known,
       Whate'er that idol be,
    Help me to tear it from thy throne
       And worship only thee.

4 So shall my walk be close with God,
       Calm and serene my frame;
    So purer light shall mark the road
       That leads me to the Lamb.

88   *W. Cowper*, 1731-1800

PASSIONTIDE

RIDE ON! RIDE ON IN MAJESTY!

Adapted from a Chorale in the *Musikalisches Handbuch*, Hamburg, 1690

RIDE on! ride on in majesty!
Hark, all the tribes hosanna cry;
Thine humble beast pursues his road
With palms and scattered garments strowed.

2 Ride on! ride on in majesty!
In lowly pomp ride on to die:
O Christ, thy triumphs now begin
O'er captive death and conquered sin.

3 Ride on! ride on in majesty!
The wingèd squadrons of the sky
Look down with sad and wondering eyes
To see the approaching sacrifice.

4 Ride on! ride on in majesty!
Thy last and fiercest strife is nigh;
The Father, on his sapphire throne,
Expects his own anointed Son.

5 Ride on! ride on in majesty!
   In lowly pomp ride on to die;
   Bow thy meek head to mortal pain,
   Then take, O God, thy power, and reign.

H. H. Milman, 1791-1868   91

THERE IS A GREEN HILL FAR AWAY

W. HORSLEY, 1774-1858

THERE is a green hill far away,
　　Without a city wall,
Where the dear Lord was crucified
　　Who died to save us all.

2　We may not know, we cannot tell,
　　　What pains he had to bear,
　　But we believe it was for us
　　　He hung and suffered there.

3　He died that we might be forgiven,
　　　He died to make us good;
　　That we might go at last to heaven,
　　　Saved by his precious blood.

4　O, dearly, dearly has he loved,
　　　And we must love him too,
　　And trust in his redeeming blood
　　　And try his works to do.

Mrs C. F. Alexander, 1818-95

WHEN I SURVEY THE WONDROUS CROSS

Adapted by E. MILLER, 1731-1807

WHEN I survey the wondrous cross,
 On which the Prince of Glory died,
My richest gain I count but loss,
 And pour contempt on all my pride.

2 Forbid it, Lord, that I should boast
 Save in the death of Christ my God;
All the vain things that charm me most,
 I sacrifice them to his blood.

3 See from his head, his hands, his feet,
 Sorrow and love flow mingled down;
Did e'er such love and sorrow meet,
 Or thorns compose so rich a crown?

4 His dying crimson, like a robe,
 Spreads o'er his body on the tree;
Then am I dead to all the globe,
 And all the globe is dead to me.

5. Were the whole realm of nature mine,
   That were a present far too small;
Love so amazing, so divine,
   Demands my soul, my life, my all.

I. Watts, (1674-1748)

95

O SACRED HEAD

Melody by H. L. HASSLER, 1564-1612. Adapted and harmonized by
J. S. BACH, 1685-1750

O SACRED head, sore wounded,
　　Defiled and put to scorn;
O kingly head, surrounded
　　With mocking crown of thorn:
What sorrow mars thy grandeur?
　　Can death thy bloom deflower?
O countenance whose splendour
　　The hosts of heaven adore!

2　Thy beauty, long-desirèd,
　　　Hath vanished from our sight;
　Thy power is all expirèd,
　　　And quenched the light of light.
　Ah me! for whom thou diest,
　　　Hide not so far thy grace:
　Show me, O Love most highest,
　　　The brightness of thy face.

3 I pray thee, Jesus, own me,
   Me, Shepherd good, for thine;
 Who to thy fold hast won me,
   And fed with truth divine.
 Me guilty, me refuse not,
   Incline thy face to me,
 This comfort that I lose not,
   On earth to comfort thee.

4 In thy most bitter passion
   My heart to share doth cry,
 With thee for my salvation
   Upon the cross to die.
 Ah, keep my heart thus movèd
   To stand thy cross beneath,
 To mourn thee, well-belovèd,
   Yet thank thee for thy death.

5 My days are few, O fail not,
   With thine immortal power,
 To hold me that I quail not
   In death's most fearful hour:
 That I may fight befriended,
   And see in my last strife
 To me thine arms extended
   Upon the cross of life.

P. Gerhardt, 1607-76, based on Salve caput
cruentatum *(probably by Arnulf von Loewen, 1200-50).*
Tr. R. Bridges

97

MY SONG IS LOVE UNKNOWN

JOHN IRELAND, 1879-1962

MY song is love unknown,
　　My Saviour's love to me,
Love to the loveless shown,
　　That they might lovely be.
　　　　O who am I,
　　　　　　That for my sake
　　　　　　My Lord should take
　　　　Frail flesh, and die?

2　He came from his blest throne,
　　　　Salvation to bestow;
　　But men made strange, and none
　　　　The longed-for Christ would know.
　　　　　　But O, my friend,
　　　　　　　　My friend indeed,
　　　　　　　　Who at my need
　　　　　　His life did spend!

3 Sometimes they strew his way,
    And his sweet praises sing;
Resounding all the day
    Hosannas to their king.
      Then 'Crucify!'
        Is all their breath,
        And for his death
      They thirst and cry.

4 Why, what hath my Lord done?
    What makes this rage and spite?
He made the lame to run,
    He gave the blind their sight.
      Sweet injuries!
        Yet they at these
        Themselves displease,
      And 'gainst him rise.

5 They rise, and needs will have
    My dear Lord made away;
A murderer they save,
    The Prince of Life they slay.
      Yet cheerful he
        To suffering goes,
        That he his foes
      From thence might free.

6 In life, no house, no home
    My Lord on earth might have;
In death, no friendly tomb
    But what a stranger gave.
      What may I say?
        Heaven was his home;
        But mine the tomb
      Wherein he lay.

7 Here might I stay and sing,
    No story so divine;
Never was love, dear King,
    Never was grief like thine.
      This is my Friend,
        In whose sweet praise
        I all my days
      Could gladly spend.

Samuel Crossman, c. 1624-84

Passiontide

ALL GLORY, LAUD, AND HONOUR

Melody by M. TESCHNER, c. 1613. Adapted and harmonized
by J. S. BACH, 1685-1750

ALL glory, laud, and honour
    To thee, Redeemer, King,
To whom the lips of children
    Made sweet hosannas ring.

2 Thou art the King of Israel,
    Thou David's royal Son,
Who in the Lord's name comest,
    The King and blessèd one:

3 The company of angels
    Are praising thee on high,
And mortal men and all things
    Created make reply:

4 The people of the Hebrews
    With palms before thee went;
Our praise and prayer and anthems
    Before thee we present:

5 To thee before thy passion
    They sang their hymns of praise
To thee now high exalted
    Our melody we raise:

6 Thou didst accept their praises:
    Accept the prayers we bring,
Who in all good delightest,
    Thou good and gracious King:

100   *Theodulph of Orleans, d. 821. Tr. J. M. Neale*

Passiontide

Were you there

Spiritual

WERE you there when they crucified my Lord?
Were you there when they crucified my Lord?
O, sometimes it causes me to tremble, tremble, tremble.
Were you there when they crucified my Lord?

2 Were you there when they nailed him to a tree?
Were you there when they nailed him to a tree?
O, sometimes it causes me to tremble, tremble, tremble.
Were you there when they nailed him to a tree?

3 Were you there when they pierced him in the side?
Were you there when they pierced him in the side?
O, sometimes it causes me to tremble, tremble, tremble.
Were you there when they pierced him in the side?

4 Were you there when the sun refused to shine?
Were you there when the sun refused to shine?
O, sometimes it causes me to tremble, tremble, tremble.
Were you there when the sun refused to shine?

5 Were you there when they laid him in the tomb?
Were you there when they laid him in the tomb?
O, sometimes it causes me to tremble, tremble, tremble.
Were you there when they laid him in the tomb?

6 Were you there when he rose from out the tomb?
Were you there when he rose from out the tomb?
O, sometimes it causes me to tremble, tremble, tremble.
Were you there when he rose from out the tomb?

DROP, DROP, SLOW TEARS

First strain of Song 46, O. GIBBONS, 1583-1625

DROP, drop, slow tears,
    And bathe those beauteous feet,
Which brought from heaven
    The news and Prince of Peace.

2 Cease not, wet eyes,
    His mercies to entreat;
To cry for vengeance
    Sin doth never cease.

3 In your deep floods
    Drown all my faults and fears;
Nor let his eye
    See sin, but through my tears.

Phineas Fletcher, 1582-1650

EASTER

THE STRIFE IS O'ER, THE BATTLE DONE

First three lines adapted from a 'Gloria Patri' by
G. P. DA PALESTRINA, 1525-94. Alleluya by W. H. MONK, 1823-89

THE strife is o'er, the battle done;
Now is the Victor's triumph won;
O let the song of praise be sung:

Alleluya!

2 Death's mightiest powers have done their worst,
And Jesus hath his foes dispersed;
Let shouts of praise and joy outburst:

3 On the third morn he rose again
Glorious in majesty to reign;
O let us swell the joyful strain:

4 Lord, by the stripes which wounded thee,
From death's dread sting thy servants free,
That we may live, and sing to thee:

Ascribed to 18th cent. Tr. F. Pott

CHRIST THE LORD IS RISEN AGAIN!

Later form of Medieval French Melody

CHRIST the Lord is risen again!
Christ hath broken every chain!
Hark, the angels shout for joy,
Singing evermore on high:

Alleluya!

2 He who gave for us his life,
   Who for us endured the strife,
   Is our Paschal lamb to-day!
   We too sing for joy, and say:

3 He who bore all pain and loss
   Comfortless upon the cross,
   Lives in glory now on high,
   Pleads for us, and hears our cry:

4 Thou, our Paschal lamb indeed,
   Christ, to-day thy people feed;
   Take our sins and guilt away,
   That we all may sing for ay:

Michael Weisse, c. 1480-1534. Tr. C. Winkworth

JESUS CHRIST IS RISEN TODAY, ALLELUYA!

Altered from melody in *Lyra Davidica*, 1708

JESUS Christ is risen to-day, Alleluya!
Our triumphant holy day, Alleluya!
Who did once, upon the cross, Alleluya!
Suffer to redeem our loss. Alleluya!

2 Hymns of praise then let us sing
Unto Christ, our heavenly King,
Who endured the cross and grave,
Sinners to redeem and save:

3 But the pains that he endured
Our salvation have procured;
Now above the sky he's King,
Where the angels ever sing:

Lyra Davidica (1708), *and the Supplement* (1816)

Jesus Lives!

German Melody, about 12th cent.

Jesus lives! thy terrors now
    Can, O death, no more appal us;
Jesus lives! by this we know
    Thou, O grave, canst not enthral us:

Alleluya!

2 Jesus lives! henceforth is death
      But the gate of life immortal;
   This shall calm our trembling breath,
      When we pass its gloomy portal:

3 Jesus lives! for us he died;
      Then, alone to Jesus living,
   Pure in heart may we abide,
      Glory to our Saviour giving:

4 Jesus lives! our hearts know well
      Nought from us his love shall sever;
   Life, nor death, nor powers of hell
      Tear us from his keeping ever:

5 Jesus lives! to him the throne
      Over all the world is given;
   May we go where he is gone,
      Rest and reign with him in heaven:

C. F. Gellert, 1715-69. Tr. F. E. Cox

ASCENSION
TIDE

Ascensiontide

THE HEAD THAT ONCE WAS CROWNED WITH THORNS

Probably by J. CLARKE, 1670-1707

THE head that once was crowned with thorns
    Is crowned with glory now:
A royal diadem adorns
    The mighty victor's brow.

2 The highest place that heaven affords
    Is his, is his by right,
The King of kings and Lord of lords,
    And heaven's eternal Light;

3 The joy of all who dwell above,
    The joy of all below,
To whom he manifests his love,
    And grants his name to know.

4 To them the cross, with all its shame,
    With all its grace, is given:
Their name an everlasting name,
    Their joy the joy of heaven.

5 They suffer with their Lord below,
    They reign with him above,
Their profit and their joy to know
    The mystery of his love.

6 The cross he bore is life and health
    Though shame and death to him
His people's hope, his people's wea
    Their everlasting theme.

T. Kelly, 1769-1854

GENERAL

GOD BE IN MY HEAD

R. O. MORRIS

GOD be in my head,
And in my understanding;

2 God be in mine eyes,
And in my looking;

3 God be in my mouth,
And in my speaking;

4 God be in my heart,
And in my thinking;

5 God be at mine end,
And at my departing.

Horae B. V. Mariae, 1514

SAY NOT 'THE STRUGGLE NAUGHT AVAILETH

Harmonized by J. S. BACH, 1685-1750

SAY not, 'The struggle nought availeth,
    The labour and the wounds are vain,
The enemy faints not, nor faileth,
    And as things have been they remain.'

2 If hopes were dupes, fears may be liars;
    It may be, in yon smoke concealed,
Your comrades chase e'en now the fliers,
    And, but for you, possess the field.

3 For while the tired waves, vainly breaking,
    Seem here no painful inch to gain,
Far back, through creeks and inlets making,
    Comes silent, flooding in, the main.

4 And not by eastern windows only,
    When daylight comes, comes in the light;
In front the sun climbs slow, how slowly,
    But westward, look, the land is bright!

      Arthur Hugh Clough, 1819-61

ALL PEOPLE THAT ON EARTH DO DWELL

Melody from *Genevan Psalter*, 1551

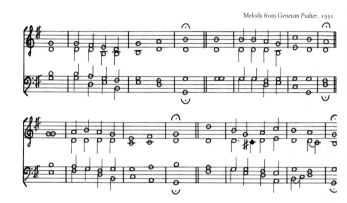

ALL people that on earth do dwell,
    Sing to the Lord with cheerful voice;
Him serve with mirth, his praise forth tell,
    Come ye before him, and rejoice.

2 The Lord, ye know, is God indeed;
    Without our aid he did us make;
We are his folk, he doth us feed,
    And for his sheep he doth us take.

3 O enter then his gates with praise;
    Approach with joy his courts unto;
Praise, laud, and bless his name always,
    For it is seemly so to do.

4 For why, the Lord our God is good:
    His mercy is for ever sure;
His truth at all times firmly stood,
    And shall from age to age endure.

5 To Father, Son, and Holy Ghost,
    The God whom heaven and earth adore,
From men and from the angel-host
    Be praise and glory evermore.

W. Kethe, Daye's Psalter (1560-1), and
Scottish Psalter (1650)

NEARER, MY GOD, TO THEE

GEOFFREY SHAW, 1879-1943

NEARER, my God, to thee,
        Nearer to thee!
E'en though it be a cross
        That raiseth me,
Still all my song would be,
'Nearer, my God, to thee,
        Nearer to thee!'

2   Though, like the wanderer,
        The sun gone down,
    Darkness be over me,
        My rest a stone;
    Yet in my dreams I'd be
    Nearer, my God, to thee,
        Nearer to thee.

3 There let the way appear
   Steps unto heaven;
All that thou send'st to me
   In mercy given,
Angels to beckon me
Nearer, my God, to thee,
   Nearer to thee.

4 Then, with my waking thoughts
   Bright with thy praise,
Out of my stony griefs
   Beth-el I'll raise;
So by my woes to be
Nearer, my God, to thee,
   Nearer to thee.

5 Or if on joyful wing
   Cleaving the sky,
Sun, moon, and stars forgot,
   Upwards I fly,
Still all my song shall be,
'Nearer, my God, to thee,
   Nearer to thee!'

Mrs Sarah F. Adams, 1805-48

THERE IS A BOOK WHO RUNS MAY READ

T. TALLIS, *c.* 1510-85

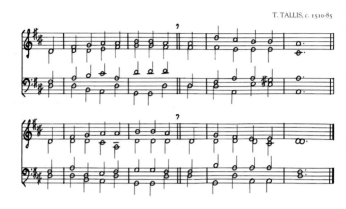

THERE is a book who runs may read,
    Which heavenly truth imparts;
And all the lore its scholars need,
    Pure eyes and Christian hearts.

2 The works of God, above, below,
    Within us and around,
  Are pages in that book, to show
    How God himself is found.

3 The glorious sky, embracing all,
    Is like the Maker's love,
  Wherewith encompassed, great and small
    In peace and order move.

4 The moon above, the Church below,
    A wondrous race they run;
  But all their radiance, all their glow,
    Each borrows of its sun.

5 The raging fire, the roaring wind,
    Thy boundless power display;
  But in the gentler breeze we find
    Thy Spirit's viewless way.

6 Two worlds are ours: 'tis only sin
    Forbids us to descry
 The mystic heaven and earth within,
    Plain as the sea and sky.

7 Thou, who hast given me eyes to see
    And love this sight so fair,
   Give me a heart to find out thee,
    And read thee everywhere.

J. Keble, 1792-1866

FATHER, HEAR THE PRAYER WE OFFER

J. L. STEINER, 1688-1761

FATHER, hear the prayer we offer:
　　Not for ease that prayer shall be,
But for strength that we may ever
　　Live our lives courageously.

2　Not for ever in green pastures
　　　Do we ask our way to be;
　　But the steep and rugged pathway
　　　May we tread rejoicingly.

3　Not for ever by still waters
　　　Would we idly rest and stay;
　　But would smite the living fountains
　　　From the rocks along our way.

4　Be our strength in hours of weakness,
　　　In our wanderings be our guide;
　　Through endeavour, failure, danger,
　　　Father, be thou at our side.

Mrs L. M. Willis, 1824-1908, and others

130

FIGHT THE GOOD FIGHT WITH ALL THY MIGHT

J. HATTON, d. 1793

FIGHT the good fight with all thy might,
Christ is thy strength, and Christ thy right;
Lay hold on life, and it shall be
Thy joy and crown eternally.

2 Run the straight race through God's good grace,
Lift up thine eyes, and seek his face;
Life with its way before us lies,
Christ is the path, and Christ the prize.

3 Cast care aside, upon thy Guide
Lean, and his mercy will provide;
Lean, and the trusting soul shall prove
Christ is its life, and Christ its love.

4 Faint not nor fear, his arms are near,
He changeth not, and thou art dear;
Only believe, and thou shalt see
That Christ is all in all to thee.

J. S. B. Monsell, 1811-75

O GOD, OUR HELP IN AGES PAST

Melody from the Supplement to the New Version, 1708.
Probably by W. CROFT, 1678-1727

O GOD, our help in ages past,
  Our hope for years to come,
Our shelter from the stormy blast,
  And our eternal home;

2 Under the shadow of thy throne
    Thy saints have dwelt secure;
  Sufficient is thine arm alone,
    And our defence is sure.

3 Before the hills in order stood,
    Or earth received her frame,
  From everlasting thou art God,
    To endless years the same.

4 A thousand ages in thy sight
    Are like an evening gone,
  Short as the watch that ends the night
    Before the rising sun.

5 Time, like an ever-rolling stream,
    Bears all its sons away;
  They fly forgotten, as a dream
    Dies at the opening day.

6 O God, our help in ages past,
    Our hope for years to come,
  Be thou our guard while troubles last,
    And our eternal home.

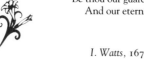

I. Watts, 1674-1748

ALL THINGS BRIGHT AND BEAUTIFUL

Adapted from an English Traditional Melody by MARTIN SHAW, 1875-1958

*A*LL things bright and beautiful,
    All creatures great and small,
All things wise and wonderful,
    The Lord God made them all.

2 Each little flower that opens,
        Each little bird that sings,
    He made their glowing colours,
        He made their tiny wings:

3 The purple-headed mountain,
        The river running by,
    The sunset and the morning,
        That brightens up the sky:

4 The cold wind in the winter,
        The pleasant summer sun,
    The ripe fruits in the garden,
        He made them every one:

5 The tall trees in the greenwood,
        The meadows for our play,
    The rushes by the water
        To gather every day:

6 He gave us eyes to see them,
        And lips that we might tell
    How great is God Almighty,
        Who has made all things well.

Mrs C. F. Alexander, 1818-95

LEAD, KINDLY LIGHT, AMID THE ENCIRCLING GLOOM

J. B. DYKES, 1823-76

LEAD, kindly Light, amid the encircling gloom,
  Lead thou me on;
The night is dark, and I am far from home,
  Lead thou me on.
Keep thou my feet; I do not ask to see
The distant scene; one step enough for me.

2 I was not ever thus, nor prayed that thou
   Should'st lead me on;
I loved to choose and see my path; but now
   Lead thou me on.
I loved the garish day, and, spite of fears,
Pride ruled my will: remember not past years.

3 So long thy power hath blest me, sure it still
   Will lead me on
O'er moor and fen, o'er crag and torrent, till
   The night is gone,
And with the morn those angel faces smile,
Which I have loved long since, and lost awhile.

J. H. Newman, 1801-90

General

138

GOD MOVES IN A MYSTERIOUS WAY

Playford's Psalms, 1671. Adapted from NEWTOUN in
Scottish Psalter, 1635

GOD moves in a mysterious way
His wonders to perform;
He plants his footsteps in the sea,
And rides upon the storm.

2 Deep in unfathomable mines
Of never-failing skill
He treasures up his bright designs,
And works his sovran will.

3 Ye fearful saints, fresh courage take,
The clouds ye so much dread
Are big with mercy, and shall break
In blessings on your head.

4 Judge not the Lord by feeble sense,
But trust him for his grace;
Behind a frowning providence
He hides a smiling face.

5 His purposes will ripen fast,
Unfolding every hour;
The bud may have a bitter taste,
But sweet will be the flower.

6 Blind unbelief is sure to err,
And scan his work in vain;
God is his own interpreter,
And he will make it plain.

W. Cowper, 1731-1800

139

STAND UP, STAND UP FOR JESUS

C. ARMSTRONG GIBBS, 1889-1960

STAND up, stand up for Jesus,
　Ye soldiers of the cross!
Lift high his royal banner;
　It must not suffer loss.
From victory unto victory
　His army he shall lead,
Till every foe is vanquished,
　And Christ is Lord indeed.

2　Stand up, stand up for Jesus!
　　The solemn watchword hear:
If while ye sleep he suffers,
　Away with shame and fear;
Where'er ye meet with evil,
　Within you or without,
Charge for the God of freedom,
　And put the foe to rout.

3 Stand up, stand up for Jesus!
    The trumpet call obey:
Forth to the mighty conflict
    In this his glorious day.
Ye that are men now serve him
    Against unnumbered foes;
Let courage rise with danger,
    And strength to strength oppose.

4 Stand up, stand up for Jesus!
    Stand in his strength alone;
The arm of flesh will fail you,
    Ye dare not trust your own.
Put on the Gospel armour,
    Each piece put on with prayer;
Where duty calls or danger,
    Be never wanting there!

5 Stand up, stand up for Jesus!
    The strife will not be long;
This day the noise of battle,
    The next the victor's song.
To him that overcometh
    A crown of life shall be;
He with the King of Glory
    Shall reign eternally.

G. Duffield, 1818-88

GLORIOUS THINGS OF THEE ARE SPOKEN

F. J. HAYDN, 1732-1809

GLORIOUS things of thee are spoken,
 Sion, city of our God!
He whose word cannot be broken
 Formed thee for his own abode:
On the Rock of Ages founded,
 What can shake thy sure repose?
With salvation's walls surrounded,
 Thou may'st smile at all thy foes.

See, the streams of living waters,
 Springing from eternal love,
Well supply thy sons and daughters,
 And all fear of want remove.
Who can faint while such a river
 Ever flows their thirst to assuage–
Grace which, like the Lord the giver,
 Never fails from age to age?

3 Saviour, if of Sion's city
 I, through grace, a member am,
Let the world deride or pity,
 I will glory in thy name:
Fading is the worldling's pleasure,
 All his boasted pomp and show;
Solid joys and lasting treasure
 None but Sion's children know.

J. Newton, 1725-1807   143

IMMORTAL, INVISIBLE, GOD ONLY WISE

Welsh Hymn Melody

IMMORTAL, invisible, God only wise,
In light inaccessible hid from our eyes,
Most blessèd, most glorious, the ancient of days,
Almighty, victorious, thy great name we praise.

2 Unresting, unhasting, and silent as light,
   Nor wanting, nor wasting, thou rulest in might;
   Thy justice like mountains high soaring above,
   Thy clouds which are fountains of goodness and love.

3 To all life thou givest, to both great and small;
   In all life thou livest, the true life of all;
   We blossom and flourish as leaves on the tree,
   And wither and perish; but nought changeth thee.

4 Great Father of glory, pure Father of light,
   Thine angels adore thee, all veiling their sight;
   All laud we would render: O help us to see
   'Tis only the splendour of light hideth thee.

144   *W. Chalmers Smith, 1824-1908*

145

IT'S ME, O LORD (STANDING IN THE NEED OF PRAYER)

Spiritual

IT'S me, it's me, it's me, O Lord,
standing in the need of prayer.
It's me, it's me, O Lord,
standing in the need of prayer.

2 Not my brother or my sister,
   but it's me, O Lord,
   standing in the need of prayer.
   Not my brother or my sister,
   but it's me, O Lord,
   standing in the need of prayer.

3 Not my mother or my father,
   but it's me, O Lord,
   standing in the need of prayer.
   Not my mother or my father,
   but it's me, O Lord,
   standing in the need of prayer.

4 Not the stranger or my neighbour,
   but it's me, O Lord,
   standing in the need of prayer.
   Not the stranger or my neighbour,
   but it's me, O Lord,
   standing in the need of prayer.

147

English Traditional Carol (from *Sandys' Collection*, 1833)

TEACH me, my God and King,
    In all things thee to see,
And what I do in anything
    To do it as for thee.

2 A man that looks on glass,
        On it may stay his eye;
    Or if he pleaseth, through it pass,
        And then the heaven espy.

3 All may of thee partake;
        Nothing can be so mean,
    Which with this tincture, 'for thy sake,'
        Will not grow bright and clean.

4 A servant with this clause
        Makes drudgery divine;
    Who sweeps a room, as for thy laws,
        Makes that and the action fine.

5 This is the famous stone
        That turneth all to gold;
    For that which God doth touch and own
        Cannot for less be told.

George Herbert, 1593-1633

148

JERUSALEM

C. HUBERT H. PARRY, 1848-1918

General

A ND did those feet in ancient time
    Walk upon England's mountains green?
And was the holy Lamb of God
    On England's pleasant pastures seen?
And did the countenance divine
    Shine forth upon our clouded hills?
And was Jerusalem builded here
    Among those dark satanic mills?

2 Bring me my bow of burning gold!
    Bring me my arrows of desire!
Bring me my spear! O clouds, unfold!
    Bring me my chariot of fire!
I will not cease from mental fight,
    Nor shall my sword sleep in my hand,
Till we have built Jerusalem
    In England's green and pleasant land.

William Blake, 1757-1827

HE WHO WOULD VALIANT BE

Adapted from an English Traditional Melody.

He who would valiant be
    'Gainst all disaster,
Let him in constancy
    Follow the Master.
There's no discouragement
Shall make him once relent
His first avowed intent
    To be a pilgrim.

2 Who so beset him round
        With dismal stories,
    Do but themselves confound–
        His strength the more is.
    No foes shall stay his might,
    Though he with giants fight:
    He will make good his right
        To be a pilgrim.

3 Since, Lord, thou dost defend
        Us with thy Spirit,
    We know we at the end
        Shall life inherit.
    Then fancies flee away!
    I'll fear not what men say,
    I'll labour night and day
        To be a pilgrim.

P. Dearmer, 1867-1936, after J. Bunyan, 1628-88

O WORSHIP THE KING

Probably by W. CROFT, 1678-1727

O WORSHIP the King
    All glorious above;
O gratefully sing
    His power and his love:
Our shield and defender,
    The ancient of days,
Pavilioned in splendour,
    And girded with praise.

2 O tell of his might,
    O sing of his grace,
Whose robe is the light,
    Whose canopy space.
His chariots of wrath
    The deep thunder-clouds form,
And dark is his path
    On the wings of the storm.

3 This earth, with its store
    Of wonders untold,
Almighty, thy power
    Hath founded of old;
Hath stablished it fast
    By a changeless decree,
And round it hath cast,
    Like a mantle, the sea.

4 Thy bountiful care
    What tongue can recite?
It breathes in the air,
    It shines in the light;
It streams from the hills,
    It descends to the plain,
And sweetly distils
    In the dew and the rain.

5 Frail children of dust,
    And feeble as frail,
In thee do we trust,
    Nor find thee to fail;
Thy mercies how tender,
    How firm to the end!
Our maker, defender,
    Redeemer, and friend!

6 O measureless Might,
    Ineffable Love,
While angels delight
    To hymn thee above,
Thy humbler creation,
    Though feeble their lays,
With true adoration
    Shall sing to thy praise.

Sir Robert Grant, 1779-1838

Steal away

Spiritual

STEAL away, steal away, steal away to Jesus.
Steal away, steal away home.
I ain't got long to stay here.

2 My Lord, he calls me,
   he calls me by the thunder.
   The trumpet sounds within my soul;
   I ain't got long to stay here.

3 Green trees are bending,
   the sinner stands a-trembling.
   The trumpet sounds within my soul;
   I ain't got long to stay here.

4 My Lord, he calls me,
   he calls me by the lightning.
   The trumpet sounds within my soul;
   I ain't got long to stay here.

MINE EYES HAVE SEEN THE GLORY OF THE COMING OF THE LORD

MARTIN SHAW, 1875-1958

MINE eyes have seen the glory of the coming of the Lord;
He is trampling out the vintage where the grapes of wrath are
stored;
He hath loosed the fateful lightning of his terrible swift
sword:
His Truth is marching on.

2 I have seen him in the watch-fires of a hundred circling
    camps;
  They have builded him an altar in the evening dews and damps;
  I have read his righteous sentence by the dim and flaring
    lamps:
  His Day is marching on.

3 I have read a fiery gospel, writ in burnished rows of
    steel:
  'As ye deal with my contemners, so with you my grace shall
    deal;
  Let the Hero born of woman crush the serpent with his heel,
  Since God is marching on.

4 He has sounded forth the trumpet that shall never call
    retreat;
  He is sifting out the hearts of men before his judgment-seat;
  O be swift, my soul, to answer him; be jubilant, my feet!
  Our God is marching on.

5 In the beauty of the lilies Christ was born across the sea,
  With a glory in his bosom that transfigures you and me;
  As he died to make men holy, let us die to make men free,
  While God is marching on.

6 He is coming like the glory of the morning on the wave;
  He is wisdom to the mighty, he is succour to the brave;
  So the world shall be his foot-stool, and the soul of time
    his slave:
  Our God is marching on.

Mrs Julia Ward Howe, 1819-1910

MY SOUL, THERE IS A COUNTRY

Melody by MELCHIOR VULPIUS, c. 1560-1616. Adapted and
harmonized by J. S. BACH, 1685-1750

MY soul, there is a country
    Far beyond the stars,
Where stands a wingèd sentry
    All skilful in the wars:

2 There above noise, and danger,
    Sweet peace sits crowned with smiles,
 And one born in a manger
    Commands the beauteous files.

3 He is thy gracious friend,
    And – O my soul, awake! –
 Did in pure love descend,
    To die here for thy sake.

4 If thou canst get but thither,
    There grows the flower of peace,
 The Rose that cannot wither,
    Thy fortress and thy ease.

5 Leave then thy foolish ranges,
    For none can thee secure
 But one, who never changes,
    Thy God, thy life, thy cure.

Henry Vaughan the Silurist, 1622-95

As pants the hart for cooling streams

R. A. SMITH'S *Sacred Music*, 1825

As pants the hart for cooling streams
  When heated in the chase,
So longs my soul, O God, for thee,
  And thy refreshing grace.

2 For thee, my God, the living God,
    My thirsty soul doth pine:
  O when shall I behold thy face,
    Thou Majesty divine?

3 Why restless, why cast down, my soul?
    Hope still, and thou shalt sing
  The praise of him who is thy God,
    Thy health's eternal spring.

4 To Father, Son, and Holy Ghost,
    The God whom we adore,
  Be glory, as it was, is now,
    And shall be evermore.

N. Tate and N. Brady, New Version (1696)

DEVS QVI

165

I VOW TO THEE, MY COUNTRY

GUSTAV HOLST, 1874-1934

I VOW to thee, my country, all earthly things above,
Entire and whole and perfect, the service of my love;
The love that asks no question, the love that stands the test,
That lays upon the altar the dearest and the best;
The love that never falters, the love that pays the price,
The love that makes undaunted the final sacrifice.

2 And there's another country, I've heard of long ago,
Most dear to them that love her, most great to them that know;
We may not count her armies, we may not see her King;
Her fortress is a faithful heart, her pride is suffering;
And soul by soul and silently her shining bounds increase,
And her ways are ways of gentleness and all her paths are peace.

Sir Cecil Spring Rice, 1859-1918

LET ALL THE WORLD IN EVERY CORNER SING

MARTIN SHAW, 1875-1958

LET all the world in every corner sing,
My God and King!
The heavens are not too high,
His praise may thither fly;
The earth is not too low,
His praises there may grow.
Let all the world in every corner sing,
My God and King!

2 Let all the world in every corner sing,
   My God and King!
   The Church with psalms must shout,
   No door can keep them out;
   But, above all, the heart
   Must bear the longest part.
 Let all the world in every corner sing,
   My God and King!

George Herbert, 1593-1633

THE KING OF LOVE MY SHEPHERD IS

Ancient Irish Hymn Melody (Original form)

THE King of love my shepherd is,
    Whose goodness faileth never;
I nothing lack if I am his
    And he is mine for ever.

2 Where streams of living water flow
    My ransomed soul he leadeth,
And where the verdant pastures grow
    With food celestial feedeth.

3 Perverse and foolish oft I strayed,
    But yet in love he sought me,
And on his shoulder gently laid,
    And home, rejoicing, brought me.

4 In death's dark vale I fear no ill
    With thee, dear Lord, beside me;
Thy rod and staff my comfort still,
    Thy cross before to guide me.

5 Thou spread'st a table in my sight;
    Thy unction grace bestoweth:
  And O what transport of delight
    From thy pure chalice floweth!

6 And so through all the length of days
    Thy goodness faileth never;
  Good Shepherd, may I sing thy praise
    Within thy house for ever.

Sir H. W. Baker, 1821-77

JESUS, PRICELESS TREASURE

German Traditional Melody adapted by J. CRÜGER, 1598-1662.
Further adapted and harmonized by J. S. BACH, 1685-1750

JESUS, priceless treasure,
Source of purest pleasure,
  Truest friend to me;
Long my heart hath panted,
Till it well-nigh fainted,
  Thirsting after thee.
Thine I am, O spotless Lamb,
I will suffer nought to hide thee,
  Ask for nought beside thee.

2 In thine arm I rest me;
   Foes who would molest me
       Cannot reach me here.
   Though the earth be shaking,
   Every heart be quaking,
       God dispels our fear;
   Sin and hell in conflict fell
   With their heaviest storms assail us:
       Jesus will not fail us.

3 Hence, all thoughts of sadness!
   For the Lord of gladness,
       Jesus, enters in:
   Those who love the Father,
   Though the storms may gather,
       Still have peace within;
   Yea, what'er we here must bear,
   Still in thee lies purest pleasure,
       Jesus, priceless treasure!

J. Franck, 1618-77. Tr. C. Winkworth

DEAR LORD AND FATHER OF MANKIND

C. HUBERT H. PARRY, 1848-1918 (from *Judith*).

DEAR Lord and Father of mankind,
      Forgive our foolish ways!
Re-clothe us in our rightful mind,
In purer lives thy service find,
      In deeper reverence praise.

2 In simple trust like theirs who heard,
      Beside the Syrian sea,
   The gracious calling of the Lord,
   Let us, like them, without a word
      Rise up and follow thee.

3 O Sabbath rest by Galilee!
      O calm of hills above,
   Where Jesus knelt to share with thee
   The silence of eternity,
      Interpreted by love!

4 Drop thy still dews of quietness,
      Till all our strivings cease;
   Take from our souls the strain and stress,
   And let our ordered lives confess
      The beauty of thy peace.

5 Breathe through the heats of our desire
      Thy coolness and thy balm;
   Let sense be dumb, let flesh retire;
   Speak through the earthquake, wind, and fire,
      O still small voice of calm!

J. G. Whittier, 1807-92   175

JESUS SHALL REIGN WHERE'ER THE SUN

Psalmodia Evangelica, 1790

JESUS shall reign where'er the sun
Does his successive journeys run;
His kingdom stretch from shore to shore
Till moons shall wax and wane no more.

2 People and realms of every tongue
Dwell on his love with sweetest song,
And infant voices shall proclaim
Their early blessings on his name.

3 Blessings abound where'er he reigns;
The prisoner leaps to lose his chains;
The weary find eternal rest,
And all the sons of want are blest.

4 Let every creature rise and bring
Peculiar honours to our King;
Angels descend with songs again,
And earth repeat the long amen.

I. Watts, 1674-1748

PRAISE, MY SOUL, THE KING OF HEAVEN

J. GOSS, 1800-80

PRAISE, my soul, the King of heaven;
  To his feet thy tribute bring.
Ransom'd, heal'd, restor'd, forgiven,
Who like me his praise should sing?

Praise him! Praise him! Praise him! Praise him!
Praise the ever-lasting King.

2 Praise him for his grace and favour
  To our fathers in distress;
  Praise him still the same for ever,
  Slow to chide, and swift to bless.

Praise him! Praise him! Praise him! Praise him!
Glorious in his faithfulness.

3 Father-like, he tends and spares us;
  Well our feeble frame he knows;
  In his hands he gently bears us,
  Rescues us from all our foes.

Praise him! Praise him! Praise him! Praise him!
Widely as his mercy flows.

4 Angels, help us to adore him;
  Ye behold him face to face;
  Sun and moon, bow down before him,
  Dwellers all in time and space.

Praise him! Praise him! Praise him! Praise him!
Praise with us the God of grace.

H. F. Lyte, 1793-1847

LEAD US, HEAVENLY FATHER, LEAD US

J. RANDALL, 1715-99

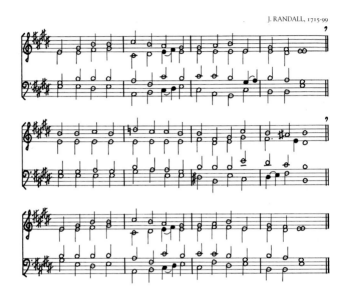

LEAD us, heavenly Father, lead us
   O'er the world's tempestuous sea;
Guard us, guide us, keep us, feed us,
   For we have no help but thee;
Yet possessing every blessing
   If our God our Father be.

2   Saviour, breathe forgiveness o'er us;
      All our weakness thou dost know,
   Thou didst tread this earth before us,
      Thou didst feel its keenest woe;
   Lone and dreary, faint and weary,
      Through the desert thou didst go.

180

3 Spirit of our God, descending,
  Fill our hearts with heavenly joy,
Love with every passion blending,
  Pleasure that can never cloy:
Thus provided, pardoned, guided,
  Nothing can our peace destroy.

J. Edmeston, 1791-1867 181

'LIFT UP YOUR HEARTS!' WE LIFT THEM, LORD, TO THEE

Welsh Hymn Melody

'LIFT up your hearts!' We lift them, Lord, to thee;
Here at thy feet none other may we see:
'Lift up your hearts!' E'en so, with one accord,
We lift them up, we lift them to the Lord.

2 Above the level of the former years,
The mire of sin, the slough of guilty fears,
The mist of doubt, the blight of love's decay,
O Lord of Light, lift all our hearts to-day!

3 Above the swamps of subterfuge and shame,
   The deeds, the thoughts, that honour may not name,
   The halting tongue that dares not tell the whole,
   O Lord of Truth, lift every Christian soul!

4 Lift every gift that thou thyself hast given;
   Low lies the best till lifted up to heaven:
   Low lie the bounding heart, the teeming brain,
   Till, sent from God, they mount to God again.

5 Then, as the trumpet-call in after years,
   'Lift up your hearts!', rings pealing in our ears,
   Still shall those hearts respond with full accord,
   'We lift them up, we lift them to the Lord!'

H. Montagu Butler, 1833-1918   183

Praise to the Lord, the Almighty

Later form of melody in *Stralsund Gesangbuch*, 1665
(as given in *The Chorale Book for England*, 1863).

Praise to the Lord, the Almighty, the King of creation;
O my soul, praise him, for he is thy health and salvation:
  Come, ye who hear,
  Brothers and sisters, draw near,
Praise him in glad adoration.

2 Praise to the Lord, who o'er all things so wondrously
reigneth,
  Shelters thee under his wings, yea, so gently sustaineth:
    Hast thou not seen?
    All that is needful hath been
  Granted in what he ordaineth.

3 Praise to the Lord, who doth prosper thy work and defend
thee;
Surely his goodness and mercy here daily attend thee:
Ponder anew
All the Almighty can do,
He who with love doth befriend thee.

4 Praise to the Lord! O let all that is in me adore him!
All that hath life and breath come now with praises before
him!
Let the amen
Sound from his people again:
Gladly for ay we adore him!

J. Neander, 1650-80. Tr. C. Winkworth, S.P.V.   185

LOVE DIVINE, ALL LOVES EXCELLING

Welsh Hymn Melody

L OVE divine, all loves excelling,
  Joy of heaven, to earth come down,
Fix in us thy humble dwelling,
  All thy faithful mercies crown.
Jesus, thou art all compassion,
  Pure unbounded love thou art;
Visit us with thy salvation,
  Enter every trembling heart.

2 Come, almighty to deliver,
    Let us all thy life receive;
  Suddenly return, and never,
    Never more thy temples leave.
  Thee we would be always blessing,
    Serve thee as thy hosts above,
  Pray, and praise thee, without ceasing,
    Glory in thy perfect love.

3 Finish then thy new creation:
    Pure and spotless let us be;
  Let us see thy great salvation,
    Perfectly restored in thee,
  Changed from glory into glory,
    Till in heaven we take our place,
  Till we cast our crowns before thee,
    Lost in wonder, love, and praise.

C. Wesley, 1707-88

REJOICE! THE LORD IS KING

G.F. HANDEL, 1685-1759

REJOICE! The Lord is King,
　　Your Lord and King adore;
Mortals, give thanks and sing,
　　And triumph evermore:

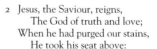

Lift up your heart, lift up your voice;
Rejoice, again I say, rejoice.

2　Jesus, the Saviour, reigns,
　　　The God of truth and love;
　　When he had purged our stains,
　　　He took his seat above:

3　His kingdom cannot fail;
　　　He rules o'er earth and heaven;
　　The keys of death and hell
　　　Are to our Jesus given:

4　He sits at God's right hand
　　　Till all his foes submit,
　　And bow to his command,
　　　And fall beneath his feet:

　　　　C. Wesley, 1707-88

Rock of ages, cleft for me

Later form of melody by CHRISTOPH PETER, 1626-69. (slightly adapted)

Rock of ages, cleft for me,
Let me hide myself in thee;
Let the water and the blood,
From thy riven side which flowed,
Be of sin the double cure:
Cleanse me from its guilt and power.

2 Not the labours of my hands
Can fulfil thy law's demands;
Could my zeal no respite know,
Could my tears for ever flow,
All for sin could not atone:
Thou must save, and thou alone.

3 Nothing in my hand I bring;
Simply to thy cross I cling;
Naked, come to thee for dress;
Helpless, look to thee for grace;
Foul, I to the fountain fly;
Wash me, Saviour, or I die.

4 While I draw this fleeting breath,
When mine eyes are closed in death,
When I soar through tracts unknown,
See thee on thy judgment throne;
Rock of ages, cleft for me,
Let me hide myself in thee.

A. M. Toplady, 1740-78

THROUGH THE NIGHT OF DOUBT AND SORROW

MARTIN SHAW, 1875-1958

THROUGH the night of doubt and sorrow
  Onward goes the pilgrim band,
Singing songs of expectation,
  Marching to the Promised Land.

2 Clear before us through the darkness
    Gleams and burns the guiding light;
  Brother clasps the hand of brother,
    Stepping fearless through the night.

3 One the light of God's own presence
    O'er his ransomed people shed,
  Chasing far the gloom and terror,
    Brightening all the path we tread;

4 One the object of our journey,
    One the faith which never tires,
  One the earnest looking forward,
    One the hope our God inspires:

5 One the strain that lips of thousands
    Lift as from the heart of one;
  One the conflict, one the peril,
    One the march in God begun;

6 One the gladness of rejoicing
    On the far eternal shore,
  Where the one almighty Father
    Reigns in love for evermore.

B. S. Ingemann, 1789-1862. Tr. S. Baring-Gould

WHITSUNTIDE

COME DOWN, O LOVE DIVINE

R. VAUGHAN WILLIAMS, 1872-1958

C OME down, O Love divine,
    Seek thou this soul of mine,
And visit it with thine own ardour glowing;
    O Comforter, draw near,
    Within my heart appear,
And kindle it, thy holy flame bestowing.

2 O let it freely burn,
       Till earthly passions turn
   To dust and ashes in its heat consuming;
       And let thy glorious light
       Shine ever on my sight,
   And clothe me round, the while my path illuming.

3 Let holy charity
    Mine outward vesture be,
And lowliness become mine inner clothing;
    True lowliness of heart,
    Which takes the humbler part,
And o'er its own shortcomings weeps with loathing.

4 And so the yearning strong,
    With which the soul will long,
Shall far outpass the power of human telling;
    For none can guess its grace,
    Till he become the place
Wherein the Holy Spirit makes his dwelling.

Bianco da Siena, d. 1434. Tr. R. F. Littledale   193

TRINITY
SUNDAY

Trinity Sunday

Holy, Holy, Holy! Lord God Almighty!

J. B. DYKES, 1823-76

Holy, holy, holy! Lord God Almighty!
    Early in the morning our song shall rise to thee;
Holy, holy, holy! Merciful and mighty;
    God in three persons, blessèd Trinity!

2 Holy, holy, holy! All the saints adore thee,
        Casting down their golden crowns around the glassy sea;
    Cherubim and seraphim falling down before thee,
        Which wert, and art, and evermore shalt be.

3 Holy, holy, holy! Though the darkness hide thee,
        Though the eye of sinful man thy glory may not see,
    Only thou art holy, there is none beside thee
        Perfect in power, in love, and purity.

196

SCEDIT SVP CELOS TVOLAVIT SVP PENAS VENTORVM·PS·XVII·C~

DNS VHVS POSTQ LOCVTVS E ASSVTVS E ICELVM. M. VLTIMO.

4 Holy, holy, holy! Lord God Almighty!
    All thy works shall praise thy name, in earth, and sky, and sea;
  Holy, holy, holy! Merciful and mighty!
    God in three persons, blessèd Trinity!

Bishop R. Heber, 1783-1826

THE
CHURCH
IN HEAVEN

JERUSALEM THE GOLDEN

Later form of melody by A. EWING, 1830-95

JERUSALEM the golden,
    With milk and honey blest,
Beneath thy contemplation
    Sink heart and voice opprest.
I know not, O I know not,
    What social joys are there,
What radiancy of glory,
    What light beyond compare.

2 They stand, those halls of Sion,
    Conjubilant with song,
And bright with many an angel,
    And all the martyr throng;
The Prince is ever with them,
    The daylight is serene,
The pastures of the blessèd
    Are decked in glorious sheen.

3 There is the throne of David,
    And there, from care released,
The song of them that triumph,
    The shout of them that feast;
And they who, with their Leader,
    Have conquered in the fight,
For ever and for ever
    Are clad in robes of white.

4 O sweet and blessèd country,
    Shall I ever see thy face?
O sweet and blessèd country,
    Shall I ever win thy grace?
Exult, O dust and ashes!
    The Lord shall be thy part:
His only, his for ever,
    Thou shalt be, and thou art!

Bernard of Cluny, 12th cent. Tr. J. M. Neale   201

THERE IS A LAND OF PURE DELIGHT

English Traditional Melody

THERE is a land of pure delight,
    Where saints immortal reign;
Infinite day excludes the night,
    And pleasures banish pain.

2 There everlasting spring abides,
    And never-withering flowers;
Death, like a narrow sea, divides
    This heavenly land from ours.

3 Sweet fields beyond the swelling flood
    Stand dressed in living green;
So to the Jews old Canaan stood,
    While Jordan rolled between.

4 But timorous mortals start and shrink
    To cross this narrow sea,
And linger shivering on the brink,
    And fear to launch away.

5 O could we make our doubts remove,
    These gloomy doubts that rise,
And see the Canaan that we love
    With unbeclouded eyes!

6 Could we but climb where Moses stood,
    And view the landscape o'er,
Not Jordan's stream, nor death's cold flood,
    Should fright us from the shore!

I. Watts, 1674-1748

The Church in Heaven

For all the saints who from their labours rest

R. VAUGHAN WILLIAMS, 1872-1958

FOR all the saints who from their labours rest,
Who thee by faith before the world confest,
Thy name, O Jesus, be for ever blest:

Alleluya!

2 Thou wast their rock, their fortress, and their might;
Thou, Lord, their captain in the well-fought fight;
Thou in the darkness drear their one true light:

3 O may thy soldiers, faithful, true, and bold,
   Fight as the saints who nobly fought of old,
   And win, with them, the victor's crown of gold:

4 O blest communion! fellowship divine!
   We feebly struggle, they in glory shine;
   Yet all are one in thee, for all are thine:

5 And when the strife is fierce, the warfare long,
   Steals on the ear the distant triumph-song,
   And hearts are brave again, and arms are strong:

6 The golden evening brightens in the west;
   Soon, soon to faithful warriors cometh rest;
   Sweet is the calm of paradise the blest:

7 But lo! there breaks a yet more glorious day;
   The saints triumphant rise in bright array:
   The King of Glory passes on his way:

8 From earth's wide bounds, from ocean's farthest coast,
   Through gates of pearl streams in the countless host,
   Singing to Father, Son, and Holy Ghost:

Bishop W. W. How, 1823-97

The Church in Heaven

GIVE ME THE WINGS OF FAITH

Melody by ORLANDO GIBBONS, 1583-1625

GIVE me the wings of faith to rise
  Within the veil, and see
The saints above, how great their joys,
  How bright their glories be.

2 Once they were mourning here below,
    And wet their couch with tears;
  They wrestled hard, as we do now,
    With sins and doubts and fears.

3 I ask them whence their victory came;
    They, with united breath,
  Ascribe their conquest to the Lamb,
    Their triumph to his death.

4 They marked the footsteps that he trod,
    His zeal inspired their breast,
  And, following their incarnate God,
    Possess the promised rest.

5 Our glorious Leader claims our praise
    For his own pattern given;
  While the long cloud of witnesses
    Show the same path to heaven.

I. Watts, 1674-1748

THE
CHURCH
ON EARTH

THE CHURCH'S ONE FOUNDATION

Founded on a German Medieval Traditional Melody

THE Church's one foundation
   Is Jesus Christ, her Lord;
She is his new creation
   By water and the word:
From heaven he came and sought her
   To be his holy bride,
With his own blood he bought her,
   And for her life he died.

2 Elect from every nation,
    Yet one o'er all the earth,
Her charter of salvation
    One Lord, one faith, one birth;
One holy name she blesses,
    Partakes one holy food,
And to one hope she presses
    With every grace endued.

3 Though with a scornful wonder
    Men see her sore opprest,
By schisms rent asunder,
    By heresies distrest,
Yet saints their watch are keeping,
    Their cry goes up, 'How long?'
And soon the night of weeping
    Shall be the morn of song.

4 'Mid toil, and tribulation,
    And tumult of her war,
She waits the consummation
    Of peace for evermore;
Till with the vision glorious
    Her longing eyes are blest,
And the great Church victorious
    Shall be the Church at rest.

5 Yet she on earth hath union
    With God the three in One,
And mystic sweet communion
    With those whose rest is won:
O happy ones and holy!
    Lord, give us grace that we,
Like them, the meek and lowly,
    On high may dwell with thee.

S. J. Stone, 1839-1900

FOR THOSE
AT SEA

ETERNAL FATHER, STRONG TO SAVE

English Traditional Melody

✚

ETERNAL Father, strong to save,
Whose arm doth bind the restless wave,
Who bidd'st the mighty ocean deep
Its own appointed limits keep:
    O hear us when we cry to thee
    For those in peril on the sea.

✚

2 O Saviour, whose almighty word
   The winds and waves submissive heard,
   Who walkedst on the foaming deep,
   And calm amid its rage didst sleep:
       O hear us when we cry to thee
       For those in peril on the sea.

3 O sacred Spirit, who didst brood
   Upon the chaos dark and rude,
   Who bad'st its angry tumult cease,
   And gavest light and life and peace;
       O hear us when we cry to thee
       For those in peril on the sea.

4 O Trinity of love and power,
   Our brethren shield in danger's hour;
   From rock and tempest, fire and foe,
   Protect them whereso'er they go:
       And ever let there rise to thee
       Glad hymns of praise from land and sea.

W. Whiting, 1825-78

CHILDREN

LITTLE JESUS, SWEETLY SLEEP, DO NOT STIR

Melody 'Hajej Nynjej' as sung in Czechoslovakia (origin unknown)

L ITTLE Jesus, sweetly sleep, do not stir;
 We will lend a coat of fur,
  We will rock you, rock you, rock you,
  We will rock you, rock you, rock you:
 See the fur to keep you warm,
 Snugly round your tiny form.

2 Mary's little baby, sleep, sweetly sleep,
  Sleep in comfort, slumber deep;
   We will rock you, rock you, rock you,
   We will rock you, rock you, rock you:
  We will serve you all we can,
  Darling, darling little man.

Czech. Tr. O.B.C.

THANKSGIVING

NOW THANK WE ALL OUR GOD

Present form of melody by J. CRÜGER, 1598-1662

NOW thank we all our God
With heart and hands and voices,
Who wondrous things hath done,
In whom his world rejoices;
Who from our mother's arms
Hath blessed us on our way
With countless gifts of love,
And still is ours to-day.

220

2 O may this bounteous God
     Through all our life be near us,
       With ever-joyful hearts
     And blessed peace to cheer us,
       And keep us in his grace,
         And guide us when perplexed,
     And free us from all ills
       In this world and the next.

3 All praise and thanks to God
     The Father now be given,
       The Son, and him who reigns
     With them in highest heaven,
       The one eternal God,
         Whom earth and heaven adore;
     For thus it was, is now,
       And shall be evermore.

M. Rinkart, 1586-1649. Tr. C. Winkworth

O PRAISE YE THE LORD!

Melody by H. J. GAUNTLETT, 1805-76

O PRAISE ye the Lord!
   Praise him in the height;
Rejoice in his word,
   Ye angels of light;
Ye heavens, adore him
   By whom ye were made,
And worship before him,
   In brightness arrayed.

222

2 O praise ye the Lord!
 Praise him upon earth,
In tuneful accord,
 Ye sons of new birth;
Praise him who hath brought you
 His grace from above,
Praise him who hath taught you
 To sing of his love.

3 O praise ye the Lord,
 All things that give sound;
Each jubilant chord,
 Re-echo around;
Loud organs, his glory
 Forth tell in deep tone,
And sweet harp, the story
 Of what he hath done.

4 O praise ye the Lord!
 Thanksgiving and song
To him be outpoured
 All ages along:
For love in creation,
 For heaven restored,
For grace of salvation,
 O praise ye the Lord!

Sir H. W. Baker, 1821-77

PROCESSIONAL

Processional

ONWARD, CHRISTIAN SOLDIERS!

GUSTAV HOLST, 1874-1934

 Onward, Christian soldiers!
Marching as to war,
With the cross of Jesus
Going on before.
Christ the royal Master
Leads against the foe;
Forward into battle,
See, his banners go:

Onward, Christian soldiers,
Marching as to war,
With the cross of Jesus
Going on before.

2 At the sign of triumph
Satan's legions flee;
On then, Christian soldiers,
On to victory!
Hell's foundations quiver
At the shout of praise;
Brothers, lift your voices,
Loud your anthems raise:

3 Like a mighty army
Moves the Church of God;
Brothers, we are treading
Where the saints have trod;
We are not divided,
All one body we,
One in hope and doctrine,
One in charity:

4 Crowns and thrones may perish,
Kingdoms rise and wane,
But the Church of Jesus
Constant will remain;
Gates of hell can never
'Gainst that Church prevail;
We have Christ's own promise,
And that cannot fail:

5 Onward, then, ye people,
Join our happy throng,
Blend with ours your voices
In the triumph song;
Glory, laud, and honour
Unto Christ the King;
This through countless ages
Men and angels sing:

S. Baring-Gould, 1834-1924

227

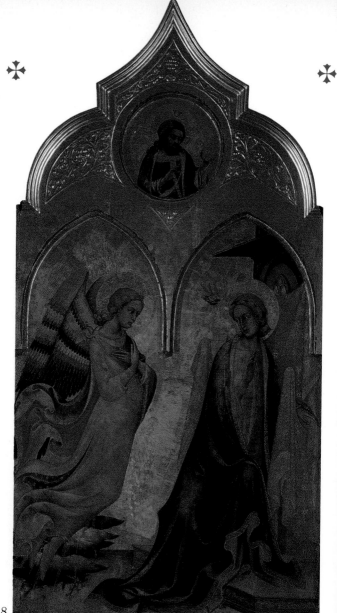

228

INDEX OF FIRST LINES

Index of First Lines

Index of First Lines

ACKNOWLEDGEMENTS

COVER PICTURE
The Last Judgement (detail)
FRA ANGELICO (1387-1455)
Scala/Museo di San Marco, Florence
(also repeated on pages 3, 13, 15, 19, 29, 35, 45, 73, 81, 89, 107, 115,
119, 191, 195, 199, 207, 211, 215, 219, 225, 229

page 2   The Mystic Nativity
SANDRO BOTTICELLI (1444-1510)
National Gallery, London

page 14   Angel Musician from the Linaioli Triptych
FRA ANGELICO (1387-1455)
Scala/Museo di San Marco, Florence

page 17   Annunciating Angel, from the Polittico dei Domenicani
FRA ANGELICO (1387-1455)
Scala/Galleria Nazionale, Perugia

page 21   Madonna and Child from the Chapel of the Magi
BENOZZO GOZZOLI (1421-1497)
Bridgeman Art Library/Palazzo Medici Riccardi, Florence

page 23   Angels from the Madonna della Melagrana (detail)
SANDRO BOTTICELLI (1444-1510)
Bridgeman Art Library/Galleria degli Uffizi, Florence

page 25   The Adoration of the Infant Jesus
FILIPINNO LIPPO (1457-1504)
Bridgeman Art Library/Hermitage Museum, St Petersburg

page 31   The Adoration of the Child with St John the Baptist and
St Romuald of Ravenna
FRA FILIPPO LIPPI (1406-1469)
Bridgeman Art Library/Galleria degli Uffizi, Florence

page 34   Initial B with Annunciation
ZANOBI DI BENEDETTO STROZZI (1412-1468)
Scala/Museo di San Marco, Florence

page 37   The Annunciation in an Initial R
DON SILVESTRO DEI GHERARDUCCI (1339-1399)   Add. Ms35,254 C
The British Library, London

page 39   Annunciation (detail)
Manuscript illumination, Edili 108, c 8 $
Scala/Biblioteca Laurenziana, Florence

233

MUSIC ACKNOWLEDGEMENTS

THE PUBLISHERS would like to thank the following, who have allowed words, tunes or arrangements which are their copyright to be included:

The John Ireland Trust, for the tune *Love Unknown* by John Ireland; David Higham Associates, for the words of *Morning has Broken* by Eleanor Farjeon (taken from *The Children's Bells*, Oxford University Press). William Elkin Music Services for the following tunes or arrangements copyright J Curwen and Sons: *Little Cornard* by Martin Shaw; *Royal Oak* by Martin Shaw; *Thaxted* by Gustav Holst; *Battle Song* by Martin Shaw; *Rothwell* by Geoffrey Shaw; *Marching* by Martin Shaw; *High Road* by Martin Shaw. Oxford University Press for the following tunes and arrangements: the music *Bunessan*, harmony by Martin Shaw; *Cranham* by Gustav Holst; *Down Ampney* by R. Vaughan Williams; *Sine Nomine* by R. Vaughan Williams; *Prince Rupert* by Gustav Holst; *Monk's Gate* collected and arranged by R. Vaughan Williams. Oxford University Press for the words to 'Ah holy Jesu, how hast thou offended', 'O gladsome light, O grace', 'O sacred head, sore wounded' translated by Robert Bridges; 'He who would valiant be' by P Dearmer and 'O come, O come Emmanuel' translated by T A Lacey.